—THE—
PROCUREMENT
BLUEPRINT

MASTERING THE PROCUREMENT FUNCTION,
AND SECURING A SEAT **AT THE TABLE**

Harold Nwariaku

The Procurement Blueprint

Mastering the Procurement Function, and Securing a Seat at the Table

Copyright © 2023 Harold Nwariaku.

All rights reserved. No part of this book may be used or reproduced in any manner without written permission except in the brief quotations embodied in other books, critical articles, or reviews.

Edited by George Verongos

Paperback
ISBN: 9798376137406

Table of Contents

Preface 1

Acknowledgements 7

Foreword 9

Introduction 13

First Things First 17

Securing a Seat at the Table: Navigating Procurement Politics 21

The Journey Begins: Lessons and Milestones 27

My Procurement Introduction: The Turning Point 33

Procurement Fundamentals Mastery: Key Concepts and Techniques 37

    My Role as Corporate Procurement Manager Strategy 41

    As Senior Procurement Manager 45

Perception Management: Building a Positive Procurement Reputation 49

Adapting to Changes in Procurement 51

    Some History of Procurement 52

Procurement Skills Evolution: Adapting to Changing Needs 55

The Art of Developing Successful Relationships 59

    Types of Stakeholders 60

        Internal Stakeholders 61

        Connected Stakeholders 65

        External Stakeholders 67

Organisations as Vehicles: A New Perspective on Business 69

Building and Developing a Procurement Team: Recruitment and Growth Strategies 73

Procurement Organisation Structure Types 74

Organisation Design Considerations 75

Right-Fitting: Choosing the Best Candidates for Your Team 79

Recruiting Experienced Hires 79

Screening 82

Aptitude Tests/Skills Assessment 83

Assessment Centres/Case Studies 83

Resumption and Settling In 86

Head of Procurement Focus Areas: Leading the Team to Success ... 89

Growth and Development: Nurturing Your Procurement Team 93

Procurement Policies and SOP Elements: Creating Guidelines for Best Practices 99

The Authority of a Comprehensive Procurement Policy 99

Contents of a Good Procurement Policy 100

Responsibilities 100

Procurement Standards 101

Self-Audit Principle 102

Document Retention 103

Separation of Duties 104

Conflict of Interest 104

Developing a Map of the Procurement Process 105

Dealing with Exceptions to the Procurement Process 107

Procurement Standard Operating Process (Sop) Guideline Sections 109

Suppliers' Information Booklet 111

Procurement Objectives: The 6 Rights for Successful Procurement 113

Crafting a Sourcing Strategy 123

Sourcing Strategy Elements 126

Business Need, Capabilities, And Objectives 126

Spend Analysis 128

Economic Analysis 130

Industry Analysis 134

Bargaining Power of Suppliers 136

Bargaining Power of Buyers 138

The Threat of New Entrants 139

The Threat of Substitutes 141

The Intensity of Competitive Rivalry 143

SWOT Analysis 144

Strengths 145

Weaknesses 147

Threats 148

Opportunities 150

Market Research 152

Competitive Analysis 153

Supplier Analysis 154

Portfolio Analysis 157

Risk Management/Mitigation 162

Sourcing Plan 164

Sourcing Plan vs. Sourcing Strategy 165

Competitive Bidding: Maximising Value for Your Organisation......167

Do you need to conduct a competitive bid for every spend item?..... 167

Skills required to determine if CB is the right approach. 168

Skills required to execute the competitive bidding process and evaluate the proposals. 170

Understanding the Competitive Bidding Process 171

Evaluation Criteria Elements 171

Evaluation Criteria Guidelines 173

Competitive Bidding – RFx types 175

Successful Negotiations...181

Negotiation – Planning... 183

Negotiation – Strategy & Tactics 184

Negotiations – BATNA 186

Total Life Cycle Costs: Understanding the True Costs of Procurement 189

Obvious Costs 190

Hidden Costs 191

Writing a Recommendation for Approval: Presenting Your Case Effectively 195

Engaging in Award Discussions with Suppliers 197

Award Discussion Guidelines:... 197

Why Do We Need to Do This?... 197

After the Award Discussion 198

Effective Contract Management: Ensuring Compliance and Performance 199
Types of Purchase Orders 199
Types of Procurement Contracts 200
Contract Terms 201
Contract Management Systems 202
Contract Management Software 203
When Is a Contract Required? 206

Supplier Performance Management: Evaluating and Improving Supplier Performance 209
Supplier Performance Management Measures 210
Supplier Performance Management Scorecard 211

Measuring Procurement Performance 213
The Importance of Measuring Performance 213
Metrics used to Evaluate Performance 215
Challenges involved in Measuring Performance 216
Best Practices for Measuring Procurement Performance 217
Balanced Scorecard 218

Embracing Future Supply Chain Technology 221
Artificial Intelligence 222
Machine Learning 225
Internet of Things (IoT) 228
Blockchain 230
Robotics 232
3D Printing 235

Procurement Analytics 237
  Procurement Automation 240
Final Thoughts and Reflections...**243**
References: 247

Preface

The typical procurement employee is a renowned firefighter.

Inundated with requests from different departments for different items and services, depending on the spend category we manage, we buy everything: from writing pens and pet food all the way to space shuttles, combat missiles, and major construction project services.

We can be many things – general purpose problem solvers to experts in specific spend areas.

We manage costs and production/service efficiency for different organisations. This means ours are usually the first phone numbers that are dialled when something external is required; time of day not being a limiting factor.

The print on popular t-shirts sold on e-commerce websites, 'Procurement manager – only because Full Time Multitasking Ninja is not an actual job title', describes the life of a professional in our field.

With or without the requisite experience, many of us are thrown into this very complex job responsibility and expected to deliver; 'After all, is it not to buy stuff?' That's what they think.

Many leaders insist, and rightly so, that ALL spend within their budgets passes through the procurement department, except, of course, salaries and allowances, thus effectively placing the responsibility for billions of naira on the laps of people with varying degrees of experience. These CEOs do not always reckon with the reality that we need to have the skills to deliver the bang for their buck, as we are typically the only outlet for spend within the organisations we operate in.

Like jugglers, we attempt to keep everything in the air; right price, right source, right place, right quantity/quality, all at the right time. This role is usually played by magicians, yet the feedback is swift and unrelenting when any one of these balls falls out of our grasp.

Most importantly, we manage people: department heads, user teams, internal and external audit representatives, vendor relationships, government agencies and regulatory bodies, our colleagues, managers, and different stakeholder groups.

What kind of training prepares us for this kind of responsibility?

As an essential function in any organisation, procurement is primarily responsible for strategic and tactical sourcing, acquiring, and managing the goods and services required for the organisation's operations.

Despite its importance, procurement professionals at different levels often struggle to secure the recognition and rewards for the contributions they make to the organisation's success.

This book, The Procurement Blueprint: Mastering the Procurement Function and Securing a Seat at the Table, aims to change that.

Drawing on my extensive experience as a procurement professional, I have developed a framework that procurement managers can use to master the procurement function and secure a seat at the table. My philosophy for success is based on what I now refer to as the 3Ps – People, Processes, Performance.

People – Nothing works without the people. So, between recruiting the right people and ensuring they have the necessary tools and development to deliver on the job, procurement managers should focus on building growth and leading mindsets in themselves and the teams they work with. Managers should provide needed development to "right-fit" the people for the tasks they are meant to deliver. This may include restructuring and team development.

Processes – If we regularly review the current processes in our organisations and reapply best-in-class processes from world-class organisations such as CIPS and ASCM, we will have established governance practices that stand the tests of rigorous audits because they are built with compensating controls and self-test mechanisms which provide assurance to management.

Performance – With the right team and efficient processes, performance is merely an outcome. Managing a diverse database of suppliers is key to achieving this. Being aware of and using digital tools and platforms that efficiently analyse data and automate repetitive tasks allows us more time to focus on decision-making and service delivery.

This procurement blueprint framework is designed to provide procurement managers with a roadmap for success. It covers all the essential aspects of procurement, from strategic planning to stakeholder management, and provides practical guidance on how to excel in each area. By following this framework, procurement managers can build the skills, competencies, and relationships necessary to deliver value to their organisations and drive their organisations' success.

	FRAMEWORK FOR MASTERING PROCUREMENT
PEOPLE	Navigating Procurement Politics Career Lessons and Milestones Starting a Career in Procurement Procurement Fundamentals Mastery: Key Concepts and Techniques Perception Management: Building a Positive Reputation Developing Successful Relationships Recruitment and Growth Strategies Right-Fitting: Choosing the Best Candidates Focus Areas for Heads of Procurement Nurturing Your Procurement Team
PROCESSES	Procurement Policies and SOP Elements: Creating Guidelines for Best Practices Sourcing Strategy Development Industry Analysis SWOT Analysis Competitive Analysis Supplier Analysis Portfolio Analysis Risk Management/Mitigation Competitive Bidding: Maximising Value for Your Organisation Successful Negotiations Understanding the True Costs of Procurement Effective Contract Management: Ensuring Compliance and Performance
PERFORMANCE	Supplier Performance Management Supplier Performance Management Measures Measuring Procurement Performance Future Supply Chain Technology tools that drive Performance:

If you manage procurement people at any level, this book is for you. However, it is also suitable for other professionals who work closely with procurement, such as finance and operations professionals. It is my hope that this book will help to elevate the procurement function and enable procurement managers to achieve the recognition and respect they deserve.

I am grateful to all the professionals who have contributed to the development of this framework over the years. I would also like to thank my colleagues and mentors who have supported and guided me throughout my career. Finally, I would like to express my appreciation to the readers of this book, and I hope that it will be a valuable resource in your journey to mastering the procurement function and securing a seat at the table.

Acknowledgements

Fuad Abdullah, you were the first person I confided in that I wanted a career change, and you were the first person to offer me the role.

Khaled Salem – during lunch at IITA Ibadan, you told me I would enjoy working in 'purchases' as it was called, and even though it wasn't easy at the start, I am glad I listened to you.

Amr Abdelkadir, you are like a big brother. I remember our dinners, trips, and time together. You remain a mentor and a friend.

You were my first manager in procurement, Karim Hassan, and what a manager you were! You made sure I got every opportunity and resource I needed to do a good job. None of this would have happened without you.

Javier Cajiga, I owe you a lifetime of apologies. This is not the place to explain, but you were more than kind to me.

Ralph Keck, thank you for your push to get me 'certified'.

Chris Brady, I will not forget working with you; I only wish we had spent more time together.

Francis Agbonlahor, in the short time we worked together, you provided leadership that I still look up to. And like you said at my exit dinner, it seemed like we had worked together for years.

Babalola Oyeleye, thank you for hiring me to work with you and for the relationship we still have many years after.

My colleagues, peers, and co-participants at all the trainings and meetings we attended together, you all played a part in forming me and making me this procurement professional turned writer.

To the teams I worked with at Procter and Gamble, Guinness Nigeria, and MTN Plc, I hope you learnt something from me; I for sure learnt a lot from each one of you.

For the multiple stakeholders I had to 'satisfy', throughout my career, it was not always easy to agree on what was WIN: WIN, but I think we sharpened each other along the way.

To all the suppliers, vendors, and partners I had the pleasure of interacting with, thank you for all you do to support organisations and to keep the 'lines running'. I appreciate you all.

My immediate and extended family have always stood with me, and you all are a big part of this.

To all of you who I call friends; your conversations, debates, and company is forever cherished.

To all who will read this book, if you learn something and can be inspired to be better at what you do, my purpose of writing it is fulfilled.

Daddy, you are always in my heart.

Mummy, thank you for constantly praying for me.

To my children, Chinwe, Ikechukwu, Nwabueze, and Nneoma, you make me humble, and I have tears in my eyes just thinking of you.

Olamide, you mean more than the world to me. You are my closest friend, and I am proud to call you my Pearl.

Foreword

In every market system, there are two key players – demand (the buyers) and supply (the sellers) – which must come together for business transaction to take place. But markets are inherently imperfect in nature, due to information asymmetry which happens when demand and supply do not have the same information, with one having more or better information than the other. The result is the inability of demand and supply to tango, for an attainment of an optimal state. So, there needs to be a perturbation to cushion optimality in the system, for demand and supply to reach an equilibrium point.

Companies are the agents which make that optimality to happen as they make it possible for the frictions (of getting products or services) which demand has, and the challenges (of reaching buyers) which supply has, to be fixed. Indeed, you are more likely to visit a restaurant when hungry in a new city over knocking at people's homes, looking for someone who has food to sell. The restaurant, a company, removes the information asymmetry problem, since both parties (the hungry person and the food seller) have a converging point, instead of each party guessing who is hungry and who is selling food in the city.

A similar scenario happens when someone has money to lend with expectation to be paid a percentage interest, even as another person (unknown to the potential lender) wants to borrow a similar amount. Without a bank, both must hopelessly wait to discover each other for a transaction to take place. But with a company (a bank), in the picture, that guesswork is not necessary, as the lender can invest the money with a bank which pays the interest, just as the bank takes the same money to lend to the borrower. What has happened here is that a bank has solved an information asymmetry problem between the two people and made a transaction equilibrium to be attained. This construct applies to all industries, including insurance, aviation, and education, as companies work to fix market frictions.

Those frictions are the market needs of customers. And to overcome them, companies acquire and deploy capabilities across many dimensions to run their operations, and effectively help customers overcome their needs.

In banking, a bank must develop capabilities in risk management, credit services, and more. In agriculture, a farmer needs to have capabilities in irrigation, harvesting techniques, and more. In insurance, the insurer must model risk and price premiums appropriately. As those components of capabilities are built, companies deepen factors of production to create products and services, which are the 'forces' which when applied on customers' frictions, overcome them. Those factors of production must be efficiently managed as they are being deployed to produce the products. And that efficiency requirement cuts across the tripod of people, processes, and tools. No business can thrive without the people, processes and tools being entwined within the production system.

Making that harmonisation activates supply chain since companies need tools (raw materials, equipment, etc) for the people to use on the processes developed within the production system. Supply chain is catalytic because commerce itself is a composite of supply chains since no company or organisation can do it all alone. You have some tools, and you need some from others, even as you are shipping the ones you created or developed to another company which needs them. As that happens, there are purchases and supplies. Indeed, there is a procurement management regime, to organise the tools the people and the processes need, to run and operate the production system.

Procurement management is a fundamental management construct in business because it manages the 'buy' activities for a firm – and that means spending its resources for the tools required for production. And since winning in markets involves effectively utilising resources, it does imply that an effective procurement strategy is supreme for companies which want to become category-kings in their markets.

When companies get procurement right, they build competitive advantage over peers and competitors.

Indeed, in our knowledge-evolving world, just as technology continues to facilitate the process of socio-economic developments, enabling new ways of exchanging information, and transacting businesses, efficiently and cheaply, effective procurement system under a broad smart supply chain management, is changing the dynamic natures of all major industries, and has provided better means of using the human and institutional capabilities of nations in both the public and private sectors, radically altering the ordinances of trade and commerce, at regional and international levels. When you buy smart, you win, as a government, company, or a citizen!

And that buying smart looks at the spaces of price, source, time, place, quantity, and quality. In this book, *'THE PROCUREMENT BLUEPRINT: Mastering the Procurement Function, and Securing a Seat at the Table'*, Harold Nwariaku explains the mechanics of a winning procurement playbook, for organisations of all sizes, geographies, structures, and growth levels. It also reveals the procurement function, and how professionals can acquire and develop capabilities, to become *masters* of one of the most important domains of market systems.

Prof Ndubuisi Ekekwe

Lead Faculty, Tekedia Institute

Boston, USA

Introduction

Experts write.

This is the fundamental principle that has inspired this book. When you successfully conquer the 'imposter syndrome' and do something you've always doubted you could do, you mostly find out that it wasn't so hard after all.

Amidst the plethora of material written about procurement and how the function should be set up and managed, I have decided to contribute my experience and knowledge to the pool. It may not move the needle in the larger scheme of things, but it will make a difference to people who find themselves stuck with a huge responsibility for company spend and don't know where to begin.

This is not an academic treatise; however, references are included for copyright attribution. The contents of this material do not contain a lot of procurement jargon or complex terms and principles; indeed, I can refer you to countless articles and materials that propose and prove those theories and how they work. I have simply documented my career journey and experiences and the lessons I gleaned working in this industry.

Our profession is such that academics do all the writing, and those with field experience never have time to document their stories. It is my hope that sharing my account with some opinions sprinkled here and there will make interesting reading for those who will take the time.

The dynamic nature of the global business landscape, and the seismic changes the pandemic has introduced to the way we do procurement, have already ensured that some of what you will read will be outdated by the time you hold this in your hands or listen to the audiobook.

Therefore, narrating my account gives some context to the doctrines I try to expound here. It then becomes easy for managers in similar situations to explore the options available to them and make decisions that maximise the benefits to their teams.

Do bear in mind that we are often caught between two categories of critical stakeholders – our user departments (internal organisation) and our suppliers (the external organisation). We are sometimes pulled in different directions to the extent that our allegiance is questioned. Many procurement people have heard the dreaded question, 'Are you working for the suppliers or for us?' We usually hear this question when we find ourselves trying to take a stand when, in our assessment, the suppliers are being treated unfairly.

The maturity required to deal with such situations only comes with experience. I try to explain how applying the principles of stakeholder management removes the element of bias and gives you some room to operate without having your motives challenged at every turn.

As you will find throughout this book, I suggest that our job is primarily relationship management. When we have developed our skills such that we are comfortable with our abilities and competence at work, what we really spend a lot of our time doing is managing the expectations of the different entities who depend on us for optimal service. Satisfying these interested parties across the spectrum becomes the yardstick by which we are measured.

In the end, no one will tell our story if we don't tell it ourselves, so here goes my attempt at doing so, and I hope it inspires someone to tell theirs.

With that said, let me welcome you to The Procurement Blueprint: Mastering the Procurement Function and Securing a Seat at the Table.

The book begins with a discussion of the importance of securing a seat at the table and navigating procurement politics. I share lessons learned from my early career and the turning point that led me to pursue procurement as a profession. I then cover procurement fundamentals, including key concepts and techniques, before delving into my career roles as a corporate procurement manager and senior procurement manager.

Perception management and building a positive procurement reputation are essential for procurement professionals, and I provide some guidance on how to do this effectively. Adapting to changes in procurement, including the evolution of procurement skills and developing successful relationships with stakeholders, is also covered.

I explore different procurement organisation structures and recruitment strategies for building and developing a strong procurement team. Procurement policies and standard operating processes (SOPs) are crucial for successful procurement operations, and I suggest guidelines for creating effective policies and processes.

Crafting a sourcing strategy and conducting competitive bidding are critical components of procurement, and I provide a detailed explanation of each. Total life cycle costs, writing a recommendation for approval, and effective contract management is also covered in depth.

Supplier performance management and the importance of embracing future supply chain technology are discussed. I conclude with my reflections and thoughts on the future and our relevance as a profession.

First Things First

This moment was always going to come.

Writing a book about managing the procurement function is like documenting my career story, and though I did think about doing this, I never calculated that it would come about this way.

I was asked to deliver a lecture as a member of the Tekedia Institute faculty, and though it took me a while to put my thoughts together, I finally did. A week after I sent in my lecture notes, I had to show evidence of why I considered myself an authority in this field (part of the requirements for another application), and I realised that it was time. This is in addition to requests from several people who have asked me to document my unique style of managing procurement.

It is interesting to note that the subject 'management' is universal. Indeed, there are many more qualified subject matter experts on either subject. Within the context of managing procurement, however, we are faced with a dilemma:

Many of the people who have managed procurement functions do not retire from such jobs to write books. A good number of them set up consulting agencies, like me, and carry on the work of providing top-quality services to the private and public sectors. We are so passionate about our work that we almost never want to leave it entirely.

Much of the material in our industry is written by people in academia, and rightly so. These people have scanned almost every reputable source of knowledge across the globe and distilled that complex world of information into clear and concise thoughts for our benefit.

Managing procurement is not something you master through reading; it is something you get better at through practice. By the time you're in a position where the responsibility for spend management and people development sits with you, you usually do not have time to read. You're so immersed in work that you do not have time for much else.

Lastly, a lot of the material available in the knowledge space teaches you procurement – its principles and strategies. There's not a lot of content that provides guidance on how to efficiently manage the people within the procurement department or function.

My experience is unique in the following aspects:

I stumbled upon the profession. My background was in business development and project management, and my foray into procurement was because of circumstances or fate if you will.

I have had to build procurement organisations almost from scratch twice, and I won an award for doing this in one of the world's greatest companies at people development.

I received some of the best training in procurement while leading a team made up of 90% new hires.

I have worked with different organisations and with different procurement teams.

I exceeded results with a relatively new team in a tough business year when few others in the company met their objectives.

I know how to deliver results with a procurement team; I know what works and what doesn't.

People write books for different reasons, and I must confess that I never saw myself as an author until a few years ago. I have always had a notebook where I put down my thoughts on everything that comes to my mind worth noting. Some of my journals are mere pieces of paper, many of which I retain in my possession: and when I do read them, I am amused or impressed by the content, mainly with how my thought process has evolved through the years and how my views on different subjects have either changed, evolved, or remained the same.

Managing people and getting the best out of them has always intrigued me, especially when I realised that so many people do not get it right.

Are procurement people unique in the way they should be managed?

I think that every individual will respond to the management style that optimises their knowledge and skills, thus guaranteeing the required performance. Procurement functions are tasked with specific requirements and expectations, and an understanding of how to bring out the best in the team is critical to success.

As I discuss these principles, I will share personal stories that affected my success or failure with the teams I've worked with. These stories are obviously one-sided, and I apologise in advance for any perceived misrepresentations or my inability to reflect the other side's experience. To protect identities, I will leave names out, but I will be as fair as possible. It is my hope that these stories will help to illustrate the challenges of managing teams in this function and provide a few lessons for people tasked with such a responsibility. I will try to highlight each lesson or insight to draw attention to it.

Securing a Seat at the Table: Navigating Procurement Politics

'If they don't promote you, promote yourself'.

This was a popular saying amongst young professionals when we started building our careers in the late 90s. At the time, the commercial banking industry was developing, and their employees would switch jobs quite frequently as they chased bigger titles and larger salaries. That was because it was easier to be promoted through sitting for interviews at another bank than to slowly ascend the hierarchy in one company. This is obviously in opposition to the school of thought in favour of digging roots and flourishing in one place; however, there are many excellent examples of such individuals. Now, I'm not taking a stand for either one or the other, as people will ultimately do whatever works for them; I am instead suggesting that colleagues in the procurement profession consider the idea as a possible path to breaking the barrier into senior management.

The phrase 'a seat at the table' refers to the idea of having a place of influence or decision-making power within an organisation. In the context of procurement leaders occupying C-suite positions, it means that procurement professionals have a role in the leadership and decision-making processes of the organisation. This could involve participating in strategic planning and decision-making discussions, contributing to the development of company policies and procedures, and representing the organisation in negotiations and discussions with external parties.

Having a seat at the table means that procurement professionals are not just tasked with executing decisions made by others but are actively involved in the creation and shaping of those decisions. It demonstrates that procurement is viewed as a valuable and important function within the organisation and that the expertise and insights of procurement professionals are valued and sought after.

For many years, I have heard this phrase used as an aspiration for procurement professionals. The way it is used suggests that we are not yet as recognised for our contributions to company success, and this may be the case in certain organisations. My view is this:

If all we do is sit at our desks and issue RFQs and manage negotiations, we are merely doing clerical/administrative work.

A buyer is a professional who is skilled and experienced at using the following tools to deliver value for his/her organisation.

Supplier Analysis: Use the 10 Cs to gather information and understand supplier capability.

Economic Analysis: Give context to transactions that take account of financial metrics and consider trends that may impact buying decisions.

Industry Analysis: Able to use insight gained from the industry to go beyond obvious costs to make recommendations cognizant of hidden costs as well.

Competitive Bidding: Apply the rules of competitive bidding to accurately request and analyse vendor submissions.

Contract Management: Manage supplier relationships effectively during and after business awards.

Policy Application: Have a good grasp of policies that act as the guardrails for every procurement action.

Just as doctors, engineers, and accountants learn the fundamentals of their profession to practice effectively, we also need to masterfully apply the principles that give our work the credibility it demands.

Doctors, for instance, spend seven to eight years on average learning about the human body and how diseases and illnesses can be treated.

After receiving their license, they keep studying to stay updated and relevant within the medical profession. When you visit a doctor, they first take your vitals (temperature and blood pressure in relation to your weight, height, and other physical observations). These data are then fed into your medical history to understand changes and significant deviations from the norm. All of this is usually done before the doctor meets with you.

When you then discuss your ailment or symptoms, further questions are asked, and additional physical examinations are conducted. You may need a blood test, X-rays, or an MRI, so the doctor can diagnose a condition before prescribing appropriate treatment, which may or may not include medicine.

Lawyers do not create strategies to represent clients until they have understood ALL the facts of a case and determined that their client has a chance of winning. They listen to and document every single detail, knowing that big cases sometimes swing on small technicalities. They study past cases and bring all their experience to bear when marshalling a plan for defence or prosecution.

Auto mechanics will run multiple tests and try to simulate the fault code encountered by the vehicle owner before they begin to propose possible solutions or make up a list of replacement parts to be purchased by the client.

I can go on, but I think you get the point. We will only earn the respect that professionals deserve when we pay the price to master the craft and use established methodologies to arrive at the solutions we offer to our customers.

Now that we have attained the desired level and proven our worth, we must deal with the level of maturity in the organisations we work for. It goes without saying that the companies we work for do not always understand the value we bring. The typical path of a procurement career should lead to a chief procurement officer (CPO), who sits on the executive committee and plays a strategic role in how the organisation is run. Many organisations limit the role to a head of procurement (HOP) status, and this can be quite frustrating for many of us because the HOP title seems to limit us from achieving C-suite status.

The way out of this is to change the game. You can choose to stay at the HOP level and moan about how much more you can contribute if given the opportunity, or you can create another path for yourself. My suggestion and I've seen this work, is that you move into a more 'recognised' role in another department like operations, marketing, or finance. You might fit into any of these fields or others with relative ease, depending on your skill set.

Finance or operations would seem like more natural choices because we are already commercial experts in the categories we manage, and engaging multiple stakeholders is already a core requirement for our success. Add a few high-level certifications, and we should make the transition to a chief commercial officer/head of finance or chief operations officer position within a few years. Some have moved from marketing roles to become CEOs.

Tim Cook – the CEO of Apple, was the director of fulfilment at IBM (fulfilment/distribution is part of the logistics function), became chief operating officer (COO) at Intelligent Electronics, then vice president of corporate materials at Compaq before Steve Jobs hired him.

Apple has become a reference for excellence in supply chain and procurement practice. They seem to have developed seamless end-to-end distribution and logistics processes for their product launches and materials sourcing. In addition, the chief procurement role is one of the few that report directly to the CEO.

Alan George 'A.G'. Lafley – two-time chief executive officer of Procter and Gamble (P&G) and former executive chairman, is lauded as one of the most successful CEOs in history. He served in the US Navy as a supply officer in Japan during the Vietnam War.

David S. Taylor – Mr Taylor has built his career in the P&G product supply organisation as production manager for several P&G plants including the manufacturing facility at Mehoopany, Pennsylvania. 'This experience gave him hands-on understanding of manufacturing, logistics, engineering, and supply chain operations. He transited to marketing, where he led major brands in baby care, hair care, family care, and home care until he became chairman and CEO in 2015.

P&G is one of the best examples I can cite for a company that recognises the critical role of procurement because I worked there, and I am witness to their success at integrating the supply chain into their overall operations. I attribute this to the operations background of two of their most successful CEOs.

Other examples of supply chain leaders who moved on to CEO roles are Mary Barra of General Motors, Brian Krzanich of Intel, Fabian Garcia of Perrigo, Beth Ford (Land O'Lakes), Pier Luigi Sigismondi (Unilever), Sonia Syngal (Gap) and Gerry Smith at Lenovo. (O'Marah, 2021)

At this level, you are part of the strategic decision-making team. This is where you can begin to use that influence to elevate procurement and the larger supply chain to its rightful place. Your knowledge of the profession and your experience in navigating corporate politics will serve you well, and you will have literally fulfilled the dream of giving procurement 'a seat at the table'.

The Journey Begins: Lessons and Milestones

I started out my career as an internal auditor in a manufacturing company, where my team laid the foundation for the first-ever audit of a mid-size group of companies in south-eastern Nigeria. The CEO of this organisation hired a very experienced consultant from a top university to do the induction and provide training on conducting audits within a group. I recall that he was very knowledgeable and patient during the sessions.

I worked with a small team of very dedicated people and a manager who understood the importance of giving employees room to be their best selves; by that, I mean that he had the opposite style to micro-managing people. I did not stay in this company for very long, but it was not because of him. In fact, I almost lost an opportunity to move to a Fortune 500 company because I wanted to stay and reward my boss for being kind to me.

It is important to manage people with empathy; many managers don't know how many employees leave the organisation or stay because of their actions.

My career really kicked off with my next job, where I spent nine years growing up and finding out who I was. My first assignment was in the far north of Nigeria, and this was when I learnt how to 'sell'. My job title was key account manager (KAM), customer business development department. It involved developing different categories of retail outlets – A, B, C stores and kiosks, to become growth partners of our company. I learnt to use the PSF (persuasive selling format) and achieve DPSM (distribution, pricing, shelving, and merchandising) while covering 70–80% of customers within my region. I would spend daytime hours working with the distributor sales team and evenings making sales calls to decision-makers (store owners).

Doing this consistently for four years with long monthly road trips for meetings formed me in ways I cannot fully express. For example, communicating to non-English-speaking customers; persevering with difficult 'gatekeepers;' sending weekly sales/inventory reports; monthly performance review meetings; competing with my colleagues across other regions in the north for who was the best KAM; learning to write 'recommendations' that could make or mar your career; being ready to 'sell' myself at every opportunity; and understanding that the answer to the question 'how are you?' is not 'I'm fine', but an elevator pitch of how well the business is doing in your territory.

Wow! Those days, 'men' were formed in the field: we learnt to manage our own businesses while working with distributors. At one point, I was responsible for five states in north-western Nigeria. Driving across that vast region helped me think straight and learn to drive carefully.

I will never forget what those years taught me and how those experiences prepared me for what I did throughout the rest of my career.

Sometime in 2001-2002, there was violent unrest in parts of the North. I was caught up in the middle of all three of these incidents, and the trauma became unbearable. I'm my father's first son, you see, and that means that it fell to me to look after my siblings. It would have been very unpleasant if anything had happened to me, so I submitted a request to be transferred out of the North. This was a difficult request to grant at the time because the company ran a very lean organisation, and there were no vacancies in my department; however, a key resource who was managing a national project resigned, and there was an urgent need to fill that role.

In my four years up North, I had developed a flair for IT and using computers (this was in the late 90s). Add that skill to my experience in sales, and you had the perfect example of 'when opportunity meets preparation'.

The role required someone with sales experience and a flair for IT. I interviewed for the role and was offered the job the same day. This was an internal transfer, so all I needed to do was travel back up north to get my things, and I was set to begin a new life.

As national project manager, I took over and deployed a field sales automation initiative across distributors in Nigeria. MARS – mobile automated retail selling as it was called – involved long hotel stays and the daily grind of working with sales teams at various distributor locations to drive productivity and discipline. I received top project management training, and I worked with Microsoft Access on Windows 95, Palmtops (PDAs), and mobile printers. This was at the start of the GSM (global system for mobile communication) revolution in Nigeria, and network coverage infrastructure was just being developed. It was an exciting project because it was innovative, and it attracted a lot of attention from senior business leaders.

This was my introduction to sitting in meetings (once every quarter or during field trips by visiting leaders), making presentations and discussing the impact of a major project on business growth. I had to send in weekly project reports, sometimes containing the same information – either that the project was going well, that I was having software or hardware configuration issues, or that we were waiting for shipment of devices for a few weeks at one time.

Now that I think about it, this was my first interaction with procurement because my team back at the head office needed to place orders for Palmtops and mobile printers, and each time they routed the request through the procurement or purchasing department. I remember my frustration with the delays and not getting regular updates.

The customers (distributors) paid for the handheld devices, and I made commitments to them for project deployment. According to the project plan, sales team training and data capture would happen within a month. The rest of the period would be spent working with the van sales representatives in the field, fixing any hardware issues and reporting progress. This didn't always go as planned, as we sometimes had to wait weeks for the hardware to be delivered. Our customers were frustrated, and the project was delayed by a few weeks at a time. When I took on responsibility for procurement a few years later, I remembered this and tried to manage the expectations of my stakeholders.

Not one for following rigid routines, I was bored by the weekly project reporting requirements and missed them a few times. This project was about to be deployed in several countries simultaneously, and Nigeria was a pilot test for Sub-Saharan Africa. Senior business leaders, including a then vice president, were interested in its progress and insisted on receiving the updates. However, they rarely acknowledged my emails or gave any feedback, so I assumed they were not reading them or they just didn't care about one small project in the deserts of North Nigeria.

In a project review with a senior IT manager from South Africa, he seemed to notice my reluctance to send the reports, and his words still ring in my ears today; 'I know you think that no one reads those reports but keep sending them'.

Keep sending updates about your work; there are discussions going on that you are not a part of.

I did not know this at the time, but they were having discussions with one another, and celebrating the fact that someone was making the project work in Nigeria despite the infrastructure challenges of a poor telecommunications network, lack of constant electricity, etc. They were impressed and saw the Nigeria project as a model deployment: If MARS could work there, it would work anywhere.

During my MARS implementation with a distributor in Lagos, Nigeria, I worked out of the head office and had constant interactions with the local leadership. This was great exposure for me, even though it also revealed my inexperience. I didn't mind being vulnerable, as it was all a learning experience for me. Anyway, during one of those interactions, a senior finance manager questioned the viability of the project and wondered why distributors were being asked to pay for devices when they were not getting any benefits. I did not have enough information to respond, so the debate was taken on by my superiors. They agreed to conduct a financial assessment of the project to determine if it should be continued or scrapped, using financial data from distributors' locations where I had executed the project. Imagine my apprehension at this development. What if the data showed that the project didn't have any financial benefits?

> *Never show resistance to audits or interrogation of your work. Don't fret over stuff you can't control.*

I had no control over this audit, and as damning as the outcome may have been, I had done my work to the standards required. So I simply went about my business and trusted in the quality of my work. Note that the project had many qualitative benefits, which were acknowledged, but the finance team needed to have comfort in justifying the costs (the numbers must make sense with them). Anyway, the analysis went ahead, and the outcome was something I am forever proud of.

Using a 'control' distributor of similar size (without MARS) and another distributor where I had fully implemented the project, the finance team stripped off the impact of all other growth initiatives (sampling, brand promotions, price incentives, etc.) and compared their financials.

To my delight, the data showed that the MARS project implementation had increased van sales by +20% and distributor revenue by 14% nationally.

The credibility, visibility, and traction this created for the project are difficult to estimate; I'll just say that this earned me a promotion and boosted my career significantly.

Shortly after this, I was asked to manage the IT department at the manufacturing site. The company was transitioning to a supply network operations model, which was quite exciting for someone who wanted to pursue a career in IT. However, this person was not me, and after a year of managing SQL databases and delivering user experience, I requested a different kind of challenge.

My Procurement Introduction: The Turning Point

 *You never know what you can get until you ask.*

Yes, I admit that I felt selfish asking for a new role just three years after moving from business development, and I could have carried on with work that really wasn't fulfilling in a bid to appear content and not upset anyone. However, I was not going to be of much use to the company in that state, and I would have been forced to leave the company. I was not performing optimally, and I was not happy. No employee should continue in this situation for long.

There will be times when you feel like the work you're doing is not fulfilling, but these moments must be temporary or specific to certain projects or time frames. If you feel like this every day, you might need to have an honest discussion, first with yourself and then with a trusted colleague, ally, mentor, sponsor, or boss. If you choose to continue and swallow your pain, your performance level will drop, and you might be having a different kind of conversation.

I had a chat with a senior member of the business leadership team, and he promised to look at options. In a few weeks, I was having lunch with another superior, and he mentioned that the procurement role was vacant, as the former manager had just moved on. I asked him what the procurement job role was about because I honestly didn't have a clue. He did a brief induction and asked me to think about it. I did, and that is how the best part of my career journey began.

It is interesting to note that the company was just beginning a procurement transformation initiative, and they were searching internally for a willing resource; they were also considering bringing in an expatriate for a few years. I attended a video interview with my new manager, and I got the job.

Let me repeat that I had zero experience in procurement, zilch. My qualification was everything I had done before then.

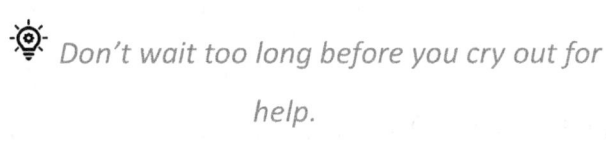
Don't wait too long before you cry out for help.

'A soccer player is only as good as his/her last game'.

If I had endured the IT role for another year, I would have had two consecutive years of below-average performance, and I would not have been a preferred candidate for such an opportunity in procurement. This is what happens when you remain unproductive because you want to play it safe. The company you work for deserves your best self, and being anything other than that is not fair to either party. Employees sometimes think that the company owes them something for the sacrifices they make; yes, they do, but it is a two-way street.

The company will not typically take a chance on a poor-performing employee unless a 'sponsor' makes a very strong case and guardrails or strict key performance indicators (KPIs) are introduced. These are done to ensure that corrective action is taken quickly and an alternative plan is implemented if desired results are not achieved within defined periods.

Because my company was taking a new approach to procurement, I had several reporting lines and key stakeholders:

Group procurement manager – based in Cairo, Egypt, who would lead the transition and take responsibility for developing me into a procurement professional. SOLID REPORTING LINE

Customer service manager – local oversight for the function. DOTTED REPORTING LINE

Director, plant operations – MAJOR STAKEHOLDER

Country general manager – overall responsibility for company operations. KEY STAKEHOLDER

I did have an interesting history with each of these managers, enough to write separate books, but since I am narrating my experience with managing the function, I will restrict this material to parts of my story that relate to that. I'll just say that my experience with each one of these superiors was unique and brought a certain balance into how my work was perceived and how I grew to manage myself and others.

Multiple reporting lines can be a good thing.

Multiple reporting lines give you the opportunity to be evaluated by different people who may have opposing views of your performance. This can be very useful when you are dealing with a difficult boss. It can also be complicated when they all think you're not meeting expectations: but having more than one person evaluate your work helps with showcasing aspects of your results and character that may be hidden from one person's view.

Procurement Fundamentals Mastery: Key Concepts and Techniques

My induction into managing the function began with a review of the organisation structure – people.

As I write this, I reflect on the slogan for my consulting practice, which I culled from my general work philosophy: people, processes, and performance. And I see clearly how this was formed. My first task as a senior procurement manager was to 'right-fit' the people.

Before this time, my experience of having subordinates was limited to distributor employees and one subordinate who worked with me on the MARS project in preparation to be my successor. Aside from that, I had not done any serious team management for the organisation.

Taking ownership of others' careers is a massive responsibility and should be taken seriously. In managing others, we are forced to deal with our own vulnerabilities, and this was my experience when I was faced with the difficult decision to inform people that they would have to look for other jobs. Fortunately, these were team members who had transferable skills, and it was easy to find places for them in other departments within the company.

Next was a recruitment exercise during which I worked closely with HR to identify suitable talents for the work ahead. I must say that recruitment and interviewing candidates is exciting work for me, and I enjoy the process of finding and hiring great talent. Scanning through CVs of potential candidates, determining what criteria to use in screening, seeing their apprehension when they first sit down in the meeting room, putting them at ease and watching their true talent shine through during the interview is something I cannot get enough of.

During my IT plant manager role, I had nominated myself as a resource for interviewing candidates, and the HR team could always count on me to make time for interviews. By doing this, I had gotten enough practice, knew what to look out for, and learned to see through candidates who were only trying to make an impression. When it was time to hire people for my department, I got all the support I needed, and I participated fully in the process. I got some of the best entry-level employees anyone could ask for, and we had an enriching journey together.

Considering that I was new to procurement, the company invested in my development. I was sent to high-quality international training, and I had the opportunity to network and interact with procurement people across the globe. I was also invited to regional procurement meetings where having an employee from Nigeria was celebrated; in many of those meetings, I was the lone but recognised voice from West Africa.

I was taught the fundamentals of procurement, and there were lots of examples and case studies from other markets. We debated, learnt, laughed, and grew with each other during those sessions, and I still have hard copies of some of those course materials. After each session, I was required to apply the skills learnt and report on the outcomes. Then I had to transfer those skills to my young team and prepare them for international courses of their own.

This is the perfect model for learning: first, you learn, and then you do while being supervised. Next, you teach, show what you do or lead by example, and observe your students and correct them. Your ability to effectively transfer knowledge is an indicator of how well you understand the subject.

Processes – because the procurement department up till that time had not been set up in line with global standards and best practices, my next assignment was to refer to standard policies and guidelines from other regions and develop a set of local documents meeting those requirements but allowing for exceptions to make our way of working easier. At first glance, this seems easy, but anyone who has had to develop procurement policies and guidelines from scratch will tell you that it's a lengthy and painstaking process.

When I requested for an external audit to be conducted, I confided in my boss that we would score poorly based on my assessment of the existing processes (or a lack of them). Remember that I had been trained on what the standards were. To his credit, he didn't agree with me; he didn't know how bad things were before he hired me, I guess. We failed the audit as I predicted, but it helped with giving me some credibility.

You might ask, 'how'? Well, when you're honest with yourself and others, and you tell the truth about your situation to the right people and under the right circumstances, it works in your favour.

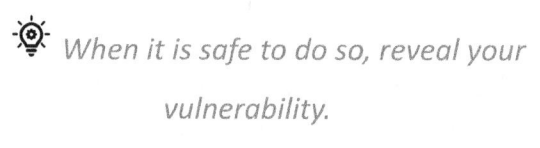
When it is safe to do so, reveal your vulnerability.

Glass is labelled fragile, so it's handled with care; a newborn baby is carried delicately. Endangered species of animals are 'protected' under the law. In the right environment and among the right people, that which makes you appear weak may give you an advantage. When it is safe to do so, reveal your vulnerability. It might give you certain 'privileges' that others do not have.

The experience I shared above was critical to building trust between my boss and me. While I agree that every boss would not manage this situation with the level of maturity that he did, it is your responsibility to determine when and to whom you show your 'weakness'. Another superior would have taken the opportunity to do me in using the failed audit results. All he had to do was communicate the poor documentation and inadequate processes as a reason for requesting a resource with more experience. This boss, however, was different and knowing this allowed me to be open with him.

With his support, I developed a set of standard operating procedures (SOPs) and attendant documents that became a template for much of the work I've done in procurement. This process took a while because of all the alignment that had to be done and the number of people who needed to have input. When it was completed and approved, however, it was and still is a document I am very proud of. As old as it is, major aspects of it are relevant today and will show procurement organisations how to set up basic SOPs that guide their operations.

Performance – with the right team in place and audit-proof processes, it was now a question of going about my work with confidence. It was easy to focus because I knew I had the framework that would allow me to perform. In the following year, I received an award for outstanding performance of any manager at my level globally. I was rated number one, which in the company was a big deal. My team delivered on all-important KPIs, and we had fun doing so.

In another instance and during a tough business year for another company that I worked with, all end-of-year parties and celebrations were cancelled because of the company's performance. It was an even more difficult year for me because I had been acting as the head of procurement with a young team. Our erstwhile boss had a petition against him (unjustly so, in our opinion) and had been suspended pending the outcome of an investigation. His absence seemed to pull us closer together, and the feeling of being 'threatened' had all of us doing everything we could to keep our stakeholders satisfied. Our thinking was, if our boss could not be spared, who were we? We worked for each other and found brilliant ways to deliver our savings numbers, service level agreements, and other objectives.

At the end of that year, I walked up to the supply chain director and demanded that we be allowed to have our team celebration since we had met and exceeded our department targets. He granted us an exceptional approval, and we had a lovely weekend bowling, playing paintball, and dining in a very expensive restaurant. I remember this result specifically because when you get people and processes right, performance is merely an outcome.

This has become the slogan for my consulting company and is a sort of mantra for me.

My Role as Corporate Procurement Manager Strategy

My next job title was corporate procurement manager-strategy, and this was an entirely different experience. I joined a company that had a robust procurement team that was well-managed. I had to win the trust of my colleagues, many of whom had spent most of their careers there and did not seem willing to go through the changes the company was proposing. Dealing with fresh graduates is one thing; having to earn the respect of older colleagues, who had a lot more experience and needed me to convince them of my proficiency, was quite another matter.

The biggest challenge with a role like this is the change in culture and the working environment. For procurement people who change jobs, this is something we always grapple with. How to quickly adapt and settle into new conditions and begin to show results within very short periods is the task we are faced with. This is not so different from any other role, it would seem, except that with procurement, there is usually a huge database of suppliers and stakeholders that you need to acquaint yourself with. While other roles restrict their interaction to suppliers within their functions, the procurement manager has to know everyone within and without the organisation.

I had a lot of help with settling in, and I remain grateful to those colleagues who showed empathy for my situation. Some of them came from other organisations and had similar experiences. I knew I had to do whatever was needed to demonstrate that I was the right choice for the role and to win over the hearts and minds of my new office mates. Moreover, I also remember why I moved, and that brings me to my next tip.

Take on new roles that give you a larger spend, not just bigger job titles.

The career path for a procurement person would usually peak at procurement director or supply chain director, or you take on wider responsibilities and grow into chief executive officer/chief operations officer. On your way there, however, the way to expand your influence is to manage more spend. A procurement manager with a one hundred million dollar spend under his/her control will most likely have more experience than a head of procurement who is managing a spend of ten million dollars.

This is not to belittle job titles, but the manager with greater spend is most likely working for a larger organisation or managing a specialist category and may have been exposed to a more complex industry. This is not always the case, so let me stick to my point: if you have to change jobs as a procurement professional, ask to know the controlled spend for the new role. If it is less than what you currently manage, you might want to look for additional responsibilities that make up for that.

My move was for a bigger spend, and a larger team, and it was well worth it. In a few months, I was immersed in the job and doing well. The company was in the middle of an SAP transition, and I was to implement the procurement module. What better opportunity than this to integrate with stakeholders, understand the business, and make valuable contributions to the project?

Not long after this, I had a new boss, and the team had to be restructured. This was the second re-organisation in my procurement career, and I think it was the most difficult. I had to develop a new organogram with a recently promoted colleague who eventually left as part of the process. None of us knew at the time, of course, but we put so much energy into it that it only seemed fair that he be allowed to stay on to implement the changes. Organisation redesigns are quite dispassionate events, however, and I remember clearly how that day went.

I was asked to engage those who would remain as part of the new structure, and my boss had the unpleasant task of sharing the bad news. We were in adjacent rooms, and I saw each face fall as the letter was opened and the news broke. With my first re-organisation, my colleagues kept their jobs, howbeit in other departments. In this case, they were asked to leave. The company did something that has set the standard for how such exercises should be conducted, though; they wrote recommendation letters to the new employers of these people to let them know that they were let go because of a re-organisation and not due to poor performance.

A small consolation to people being asked to start all over, but very helpful as it saved them having to explain why they deserve a new job if they couldn't keep the previous one.

This created gaps in the team which we decided to fill with graduate management trainees (GMTs) – graduate employees with little or no experience who are hired on an initial three-year contract, trained, and given opportunities to work. After three years, they are assessed using predefined criteria and offered full-time jobs or asked to move on. I will discuss this some more later in the book. These GMTs, as we called them, came in with a lot of energy and drive.

My approach was to have them learn their roles, engage stakeholders, and visit company locations and key suppliers without doing any procurement transactions for an initial two to three months, then ease them into real work afterwards. It seemed to frustrate them at first, but when they started managing transactions and saw how everything they had learnt in the initial three months seemed to give robust context to their work, they hit the ground 'flying'. I'm still in touch with most of them, and I can tell you that they have grown to become respected professionals in their different fields.

> 💡 *Give new procurement employees some time to settle in.*

This is a tough one for managers to follow because most operations run a lean organisation and will struggle to find other staff to carry the excess workload. I understand this, and I know how much extra work some of us had to do when we gave these new employees time to understand the roles they were to take on. I will tell you this; when they do settle in and begin to bring new insight into some long-standing problems, you will reap the fruits of that sacrifice many times over. I know how well-rounded these people became and how well they work with little supervision.

My experience with this decision was such that I could delegate work with confidence and almost never had to check back. During much of my work at this company, I was looking after my sick father. This required regular road travel to South-East Nigeria, a trip of about eight hours each way. On many such trips, I attended voice conference calls and did work with little or no interruption. I had a boss whose attitude was to get results and not monitor where people were located. I would get calls requesting me to resolve an issue or attend to an emergency. All I needed to do was to assign such work to one of my subordinates, and in a few hours, I would get a call from the requester thanking me for addressing the issue. When I look back on how this worked, I realise it was because of the quality of people we recruited, but more importantly, because I allowed them enough time to understand their job roles before rushing them into the daily firefighting that describes a lot of procurement work today.

This company had a practice of paying bonuses at the end of every fiscal year, and we all worked to earn this. I have already shared the success story of how my team was one of the few departments that beat expectations and were allowed to take the usual days off to celebrate. Experiences like that constantly remind me that the decision was the right one, and given the opportunity, I would do it again.

As Senior Procurement Manager

All good things come to an end, and in due course, I moved on to my next role, which was my last job in full-time employment. The circumstances surrounding this move are some of the most life-transforming that I have ever endured. To begin with, I lost my father a few weeks before I got the call to interview for this job, and I was in the middle of funeral preparations. I had also just done the groundbreaking for our new home, and I was dealing with a major difficulty in my marriage. Now you can imagine how overwhelmed I was, feeling pressure from all sides.

It would have been easy to drop or postpone any one of these projects, and I really considered doing so. However, I did not invite any of these on myself; life just happened, so I decided to carry on and see how things would play out. This is the reason I called this last job my 'perfect storm'. It came at a time I couldn't say no, yet I was dealing with major life challenges. I will always remember this role as one of the few times I felt powerless about doing what I knew I was capable of.

If you have followed my story so far, you will realise that I always had an opportunity to deliver results with a team I chose. There was either a restructuring or an opportunity to hire fresh talent.

This was not the case in this role; I had to work with what I had. Now when I reflect on it, I realise that I did consider abandoning ship and finding something else, but the question I asked myself was this: what if this was an opportunity to prove another aspect of my people management skills? Why did I always think that the way to achieve my goals was to re-organise? What if I was given a chance to learn something else? Looking at it this way, it made sense to learn to work with the tools I had. They say, 'it is a bad workman that quarrels with his tools', so I dug in and gave it a go.

The going was hard.

It seemed as if everything I had learned was being put to the test daily; indeed, many times, I described my experience as fighting a boxing match with my hands tied behind my back. These days I ask myself if I could have had my way by being more assertive and pushing to have it the way I was used to? Maybe yes, but what would I have learnt? I found the odds were stacked against me, yet I found the grit to push on day after day. Things I learnt from this last job are topics for procurement survival tips, and I might take the time to list them out someday.

I was able to push a major policy revamp through, though, and guess what? I used the same policy guidelines I developed in my first procurement job as the template for this. Isn't it amazing how a piece of work done with excellence can last for years and years?

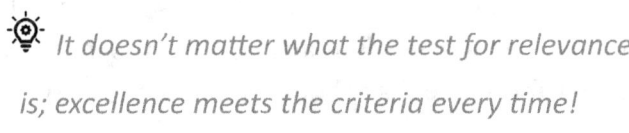

It doesn't matter what the test for relevance is; excellence meets the criteria every time!

I will ask procurement people to give this some thought as I finish narrating my experience. Everything you do as a member of this noble profession carries your signature. Do not do work 'anyhow'. Be known for class and excellence. Show that you take yourself and your work seriously. It does not matter if members of your user department appear disorganised and try to put you under pressure; you must respond with a touch of excellence and professionalism in your work. You cannot be taken seriously when your emails are poorly written, and your calculations are incorrect. When you approach your work like you have no plans to demonstrate your capability, you block off future opportunities.

What about self-development? You cannot be stuck in one place, my friends. Seek out courses and certifications that test your competence and prove your expertise. Ensure that every interaction leaves the other party feeling that they have been in the presence of a professional. This alone builds trust and credibility.

I shared my procurement career journey to give some insight and context to the thoughts that follow. It is important for people to know where I am coming from. As I discuss the elements of managing the function, I will insert more stories and experiences that help illustrate specific points. I hope you enjoy this material. I will be available for discussions and questions on any of the following handles:

LinkedIn - https://www.linkedin.com/in/haroldnwariaku

Instagram – @harold.nwariaku

Facebook Page - https://facebook.com/HaroldNwariaku

Company website – www.haroldandco.com

Foundation website – www.haroldnwariaku.com

Twitter - @HaroldNwariaku

YouTube Channel - https://www.youtube.com/@haroldnwariaku

Perception Management: Building a Positive Procurement Reputation

We do not see people as they are; we see them as we are.

I must have omitted the fact that my one outstanding trait is that I like to address the 'elephant in the room'? I prefer to confront elements that may create bias and restrict open conversations before going deep into the discussion. This is just to ensure that people don't leave the debate with thoughts that may cloud their judgement. It is no secret that people view procurement personnel with some suspicion and bias. We are exposed to a lot of undue influence and opportunities, so it is only normal to carry this cross.

There are many instances of procurement people who have betrayed the trust of their organisations and donated fodder to this bias, but there are also examples of employees who have demonstrated high levels of integrity and professionalism despite the temptations and shortcuts placed on their path. There is no statistical basis for determining the exact population, but there are also CEOs, CFOs, and members of other professions who have been lured into the same trap. I think it is unfair to place the reputational badge for corruption on procurement people without looking at the data.

Every profession has its bad eggs – accountants and finance people falsify reports, engineers take shortcuts, doctors lose licenses for mismanaging patients, Big Pharma is always under the microscope for influencing addictions, salespersons exaggerate numbers, etc.

This is not a mudslinging contest. I just want to put it out there that there's enough to go around: the bad elements in any profession do not represent the whole. I've been in this industry long enough to know that we take a bad rap for things we are not always guilty of. No one is talking about it either, so it remains there in the minds of people we work with, yet it affects everything we do. Allow me to talk about perception for a bit.

The dictionary definition of perception suggests that it has more to do with the person 'perceiving' than with the thing being 'perceived'. A CEO or CFO who has interacted with a few procurement people may have formed an opinion based on office gossip and is going to carry this perception for years to come. Every action comes under scrutiny and becomes the subject of an investigation. There is nothing wrong with this when there is enough credible evidence to support it.

It becomes a problem when even after the outcome of such an investigation finds the individual cleared of all allegations, the person remains tainted and cannot regain the trust he/she once earned. This is a perception problem and, unfortunately, lies with the 'perceiver' to fix. This discrimination sometimes goes too far and creates a burden of proof on procurement people for crimes they are not guilty of. Procurement people seem to walk around with a target on their backs and do not always get the benefit of the doubt. They choose to ignore it because talking about it might mean that one is 'guilty as charged'.

Well, if no one else will talk about it, I will; and I say that it is enough.

We are already in a high-risk profession, and this comes with the territory. I am comfortable wearing the label of good and ethical procurement, and I will be happy to engage with anyone who has a different view of us. Perceptions can be fixed if one is open to discussion. I have a recommendation for business leaders who struggle to trust procurement – hire, train, and reward the best people and review reports regularly. I will discuss this in detail later but note that good people tend to deliver on every parameter, including ethical conduct. Do not hire people who seek shortcuts because they lack the skills to resolve problems; the blowback will affect everyone and destroy your company's reputation.

If you have a perception problem with your procurement, have a discussion and get to the bottom of it. Do not let it fester.

Adapting to Changes in Procurement

It is the age of collaboration.

When we look at all the major fields of study today, we notice that they are quite different from a few years ago.

Medicine: Life expectancy has increased from 45 years in the 1850s to about 85 years today due to progress in the field of medicine. This increase in life expectancy has led to the discovery of certain diseases that come with age. Certain cardiovascular diseases and non-cardiovascular diseases like Alzheimer's were unknown in the past because people didn't live that long. Globalisation has also led to an increase in the spread of infectious diseases as travel across continents takes less than a day. This, of course, means that scientific solutions to such ailments can also be applied globally, as we saw recently with the COVID-19 vaccine.

In the USA, for instance, deaths from heart disease and strokes have decreased by 68% and 79%, respectively. An electrocardiogram or ECG was performed with the patient's limbs immersed in salt water; today, it can be done over long distances using wireless technology. Sixty years ago, congenital heart disease couldn't be diagnosed completely until after death; but foetuses can now be diagnosed with the condition, and corrective surgery is performed while it is still in the womb. (The Endlessness Evolution of Medicine, Continuous Increase in Life Expectancy and Constant Role of the Physician | Elsevier Enhanced Reader, n.d.)

Engineering: Major technological advances in engineering, from space travel to the mobile phone, provide ample evidence of the evolution in this field. The Mars rovers Opportunity and Curiosity, the Three Gorges dam in Sandouping, China measuring over two kilometres in length and producing 22,500 MW, the Burj Khalifa (almost 3000 ft high), France's Millau Viaduct, the tallest bridge in all of human civilisation, computer-aided design (CAD) software, and smartphones and Wi-Fi proliferation are all examples of how far engineering technology has advanced in our time. (Top 10 Engineering Advancements of 21st Century - Electronic Products, n.d.)

Some History of Procurement

The field of procurement has also come a long way. As far back as 2800 BC, there were records of procurement activity on clay tablets in Syria.

If items have been produced or manufactured, some form of procurement or purchasing has been carried out. In his book, *Procurement and Supply Chain Management*, Lysons identified the seven stages of its evolution thus:

Period 1: In the years before the 1900s, during the growth of the American railroad, where the procurement function was recognised as a department with a head who reported directly to the organisation's president. It is interesting to note the lack of criteria used in selecting personnel occupying the role of procurement agent.

Period 2: Up until the start of the Second World War, there were articles discussing the importance of procurement professionals and the need for clear material specifications, mainly due to war requirements.

Period 3: Interest in procurement really grew during the war years of 1940–1946. The number of schools offering procurement-related courses increased significantly, and the Association of Procurement Agents almost doubled its membership. It is also important to note that requisitions from user departments had no specific brand specifications. For procurement people, you will agree that this was a sign of the maturity of the function.

Period 4: Referred to as the quiet years, this period was marked by relative indifference to the function, as many considered it an inevitable cost of doing business. I guess that with very effective procurement teams, our relevance wanes when there are no more wars to fight.

Period 5: The concept of materials management experienced intense growth in the 60s, and some elements of the supply chain, inventory control, stores/warehousing, etc., were typically regulated by one individual. The relationship between buyers and suppliers was, however, adversarial, and not a lot of collaboration happened.

Period 6: At the close of the century, and with the rapid pace of technological growth, supply chain management took on wings and really began to fly. Competition was strong, and business leaders began to see the role of procurement as a way to manage costs and other pressures.

Period 7: Partnering with suppliers, long-term contract relationships, shared databases, lifecycle costs, and strategic cost management became the way of life post-2000. Procurement adopted a different mindset from the traditional approach to meet the challenges of the times.

Those of us who had the opportunity to join the industry in this pivotal stage have experienced first-hand the benefits of this change in outlook and what that has meant for the profession.

Procurement Skills Evolution: Adapting to Changing Needs

In a meeting with senior procurement managers many years ago, I was forced to confront the reality of how procurement people are perceived. Fully developed global organisations would typically have robust processes and skilled personnel; this may not be the case with start-ups and growing companies. Add to this the fact that experienced resources command the highest salaries and work for the best, and you have this gulf in skill sets.

The effectiveness of procurement professionals is driven by their knowledge, skills, and attitude. Knowledge can come through study and certifications; attitude is something you learn and can practice. Skills will only come when you do the work. Now take the case of a young graduate who gets hired and assigned to the procurement department. This person does not have a clue about what the job entails or what he/she is supposed to do.

For growing organisations, the structure may not allow for categorisation or well-defined processes. The procurement department may just be evolving from an administrative unit to a separate function. This individual gets thrown into the mix without training, guidance, and help. As with most companies at a similar stage of growth, the head of the team might be lacking in knowledge of procurement principles, just like the young graduate. In Nigerian jargon (made popular by the Afrobeat music maestro, the late great Fela Kuti), we call that 'double wahala', meaning double trouble.

It really does not matter how much the team struggles to satisfy the needs of their stakeholders; their inexperience will show. A team like this will stumble through the job requirements and will make lots of mistakes. How well do you think such a team will be regarded by the other business leaders? Perhaps this is where some of the wrong perceptions are formed? Even if they are dedicated to self-development and growth, they would need time to find their feet and a lot of patience from their colleagues. This is another reason why I am writing this book. I had the rare opportunity to be allowed to grow into my role with the support of great leaders. It was not all smooth sailing, but I was given a chance.

For many people in this profession and others, all we need is good fertile soil to grow. The challenges of a difficult environment or harsh terrain and their impact on professional growth cannot be accurately calculated. No farmer keeps count of how many seeds did not germinate or blossom to full capacity; instead, yield is measured by fruits. How many people are operating way below their potential capabilities because their productivity was stunted or limited by poor breeding grounds? There is no statistic to track and report this number. You either make it or you don't.

It is expected, however, that there is less of a challenge with perception issues in large organisations with mature procurement functions. Growing businesses need all the help they can get.

The Changing Role of Procurement – Developing Professional Effectiveness (Tassabehji & Moorhouse, 2008) describes the below skill categories for procurement professionals.

Technical Skills: Referred to as the core of the profession, these are the knowledge and essential capabilities required for procurement people to function. Product knowledge, total quality management, category management, cost driver analysis, etc., all fall under this category.

Interpersonal Skills: I did mention that the job of procurement will eventually be measured by how well we manage relationships, communication, group dynamics, influencing, cultural awareness, etc.

Internal Enterprise Skills: A solid grasp of how the internal organisation and relationships work, internal change management, global sourcing evaluation, and more.

External Enterprise Skills: The management of all stakeholders within the supply chain network falls within this category. Our ability to achieve a WIN/WIN with these partners is a critical factor to our success.

Strategic Business Skills: Procurement should be driving value for the organisation by managing risks, change management, and strategic partnerships.

Of all the skills listed above, my experience has shown that when procurement people make an effort to develop themselves and understand their internal and external business environment, their sphere of influence widens, and they become key members of leadership teams. Since they are usually knowledgeable in other professions (most procurement experts are experts from other careers), they combine these skills with an acute commercial sense and make themselves indispensable to their organisations.

The Art of Developing Successful Relationships

One skill that stands out, however, is the ability to manage others. Interpersonal skills, as defined earlier, are, in my opinion, the most sought-after and rewarded ability for us. For clarity, it is taught as 'stakeholder management', but in essence, it is all about how well we manage relationships. Because we are often caught between conflicting requirements, our ability to navigate the turbulent waters of 'stakeholder satisfaction' becomes critical for success in our role. How to manage supplier relationships to secure their commitment to difficult or unrealistic demands from our internal 'users', and how we persuade these internal stakeholders to accept solutions that don't exactly fit with their requirements but are for the long-term benefit of the company overall, and how to delicately balance company expectations with the restrictions placed by regulatory agencies and sustainability goals.

Being adept at influencing these relationships in the interest of the company we work for is the hallmark of a procurement professional. When looked at professionally, we can describe this skill as stakeholder management and let's look at this more closely.

Figure 1 TYPES OF STAKEHOLDERS

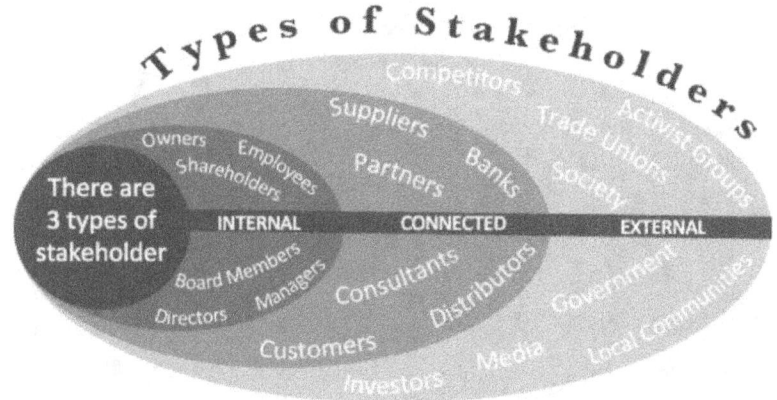

©CIPS 2020

Types of Stakeholders

The procurement professional often finds that he/she is pulled in different directions and faced with seemingly conflicting interests. The above diagram attempts to explain why this is so. It is true that when you do a strategic analysis of the outcome of these stakeholders, they all want the same thing. It is in the interest of every partner to ensure that the corporation remains in profitable existence as all their roles with regard to the entity disappear in the unfortunate case of a company failure or shutdown.

However, when you are caught up in the day-to-day firefighting of business operations, especially when you have not set up processes like I will recommend in this book, you do not see this 'big picture'. All you encounter is the flurry of requests from internal users, the complexity of dealing with difficult suppliers, and the pressure of regulatory bodies waiting for you to make one wrong step. This is like driving in a hurry; you are very likely to miss important traffic signs!

THE PROCUREMENT BLUEPRINT

Internal Stakeholders

Table 1

STAKEHOLDER	INTERESTS/NEEDS/DRIVERS	INFLUENCE/CONTRIBUTION
Directors/Managers	<ul><li>The organisation's profitability, survival, and growth.</li><li>Fulfilment of objectives and projects for which they are responsible (requiring procurement inputs and/or support).</li></ul>	<ul><li>Formal authority over planning.</li><li>Shape the commitment and motivation of staff.</li><li>Influence through politics, networking and influencing skills.</li></ul>
Staff/team members or other organisation members	<ul><li>The organisation's profitability and survival, for continued employment.</li><li>Support, information, and inputs to fulfil task goals and earn rewards.</li><li>Healthy and safe working environment.</li><li>Fair and ethical treatment.</li></ul>	<ul><li>Scarce resource: competitive edge in times or areas of skill shortage.</li><li>Threat of withdrawn labour.</li><li>Potential to add value through skilled, motivated performance, flexibility etc. (especially in services).</li></ul>
Technical/design function	<ul><li>Accurate fulfilment of specifications.</li><li>Timely, relevant, expert advice on price and availability issues.</li><li>Connection to suppliers who might contribute innovation and expertise.</li></ul>	<ul><li>Determine specifications and materials which the buyer will have to translate into purchase orders.</li></ul>
Manufacture/production/operations function	<ul><li>Right inputs at right price and right quality, delivered to right place at right time to maintain efficient flow of production.</li><li>Supplier management and SCM to support flexibility, JIT supply, innovation etc.</li><li>Sourcing and procurement services (e.g., for capital equipment) or consultancy.</li></ul>	<ul><li>Key internal customer: procurement performance measured by fulfilment of the 'five rights'.</li><li>Provision of feedback on quality of inputs to aid supplier and contract management.</li></ul>
Sales and marketing function	<ul><li>Quality, customisation, and delivery levels that will satisfy customers.</li><li>Fulfilment of promises made to customers, responsiveness to feedback, and demands.</li><li>Information on products and delivery schedules for promotions.</li></ul>	<ul><li>Provision of market research and customer feedback information to influence product specifications and quality management.</li><li>Promises made to customers via marketing communications, which</li></ul>

	• Sourcing and procurement services (e.g., printing services, office supplies, sales force cars) or consultancy (e.g., for own media space buying or agency selection).	procurement must contribute to delivering.
Finance/admin function	• Adherence to financial procedures (e.g., budgetary control, invoicing arrangements). • Notification of terms negotiated with suppliers (e.g., discounts, payment terms). • Support for cost control and/or reduction. • Provision of information for budgetary control, costing, credit control etc. • Sourcing and procurement services (e.g., for IT systems and stationery) or consultancy.	• Control or influence budget allocations. • Action payment of suppliers. • May impact on supplier relationships (e.g., if payment for supplies is late or withheld). • May be leaders or champions of cost control and reduction initiatives.
Storage and distribution (or logistics) – if not part of procurement and supply function	• Timely info about incoming and outgoing orders, for transport and storage planning. • Policies for 'green' transport planning. • Safe goods handling etc. • Sourcing and procurement services (e.g., for equipment) or consultancy.	• Control or influence timely flow of incoming and outgoing deliveries. • Influence on wastage, damage, and obsolescence of supplies (e.g., through safe, secure, efficient transport and storage).

©CIPS 2014

Senior stakeholders: One of the biggest requirements of this category is that you do not surprise them with bad news. They are not in constant interaction with the operational aspects of the procurement function, except through the head of procurement or CPO, but they are responsible for overall business results. If you work for an organisation that has procurement sitting on the leadership committee, this group of shareholders will be receiving regular updates and will cascade strategy and objectives to your team through your department head. For organisations still on this journey, you want to share monthly or quarterly reports where you detail your results, plans, big project updates, and potential issues you anticipate from the market and elsewhere. You must also build relationships such that you can receive instant access to discuss emergencies.

If the only time they are 'forced' to interact with you is when an issue has been escalated to them through another function or individual, you are not doing yourself or your team any favours. Take the initiative to 'report yourself' where you anticipate disruptions, delays, cost overruns, quality issues, etc., and share your action plans for resolution, which you must implement ruthlessly. You will have a reputation for being on top of things and will secure the trust of your superiors. You will also give the business some assurance of your capabilities and a good reason to give you a permanent invitation to the decision-making table.

Colleagues in other functions: Most of the 'user department' make up this grouping, and they are the ones we are mostly in contact with. They initiate the requests, participate in supplier evaluations and negotiations, conduct supplier assessments, provide scores for supplier performance, and follow through for work completion. As a user group, they are the most critical in the sense that they form the largest population of colleagues who will provide feedback during our stakeholder satisfaction surveys. It is therefore important that we manage them carefully.

The objective here is not to make them happy. In fact, certain decisions made in the long-term interest of the company may go against the diverse needs of this group in the short term, as you can see from the above table. The approach here is to engage them early and have a detailed understanding of what their needs are long before they come to you. With this group, if you wait until you receive a request before you act, you are already late. This is because they may not always have a robust planning cycle that factors in procurement engagement. At the time their needs become urgent, you may not have the resources or time to do a comprehensive process and deliver value. This, in turn, affects your perception and accumulates the frustration felt by everyone in the company. Another benefit of engaging early is that you will have a better view of the needs of ALL your users and, therefore, can determine exactly how you will deliver and meet their needs. Of course, there will be exceptions, but as we will discuss in a later chapter, you will have a separate process for handling those as well.

Through early engagement and regular reports of progress with their projects, you will have little reason to worry about these stakeholders, and you might begin to exit the firefighting mode you usually find yourself in. One of my reasons for writing this book is to help procurement teams implement a more strategic methodology in their work and help them stamp their authority within their organisations. Effectively managing different categories of stakeholders is one way to establish oneself as a professional with the credentials that command the respect of your peers, and it starts with this group because if you can't handle those within, how will you cope with those without?

Connected Stakeholders

Table 2

STAKEHOLDER	INTERESTS/NEEDS/DRIVERS	INFLUENCE/CONTRIBUTION
Shareholders	<ul><li>Return on investment, dividends.</li><li>Corporate governance: transparency, accountability, directors protecting their interests.</li></ul>	<ul><li>Owners and financiers of firms.</li><li>Voting power at company meetings.</li><li>Power to sell shares influencing share price, perceptions of financial markets).</li></ul>
End customers	<ul><li>Satisfaction of a complex bundle of expectations and motives for purchase leg value for money, quality, service experience - different for consumer and business or industrial buyers.</li></ul>	<ul><li>Focus of all business activity.</li><li>Source of sales revenue and profits.</li><li>Source of feedback information (via surveys, complaints etc.).</li><li>Power to switch or withdraw.</li></ul>
Intermediary customers leg agents, distributors, retail outlets)	<ul><li>Ethical, efficient trading practices and systems.</li><li>Sales support: product info, reliable supply, promotional support, sales force training.</li><li>Earnings and profits (e.g., through discount margins, fees, or commissions).</li><li>Mutually beneficial ongoing relationship.</li></ul>	<ul><li>Help to promote and distribute products.</li><li>Part of total customer value delivery system for competitive advantage.</li><li>Potential for collaborative promotion.</li><li>Source of feedback information on sales, customers, etc.</li><li>Power to withhold distribution or promotion, or to aid competitors (e.g., with exclusive distribution deals).</li></ul>
Suppliers	<ul><li>Clear specifications (fewer disputes).</li><li>Efficient transaction and relationship handling.</li><li>Fair procedures for awarding contracts.</li><li>Timely payment of debts.</li><li>Opportunities for reasonable profit-making.</li><li>Opportunities for development through regular trading, alliance, or partnership.</li><li>Feedback information to support service.</li></ul>	<ul><li>Provision of potentially key inputs (at required quality, price, time).</li><li>Power to withhold or restrict supply.</li><li>Expertise (e.g., for product development and specification).</li><li>Potential for added value (e.g., via JIT, lean supply, collaborative waste reduction, continuous improvement).</li></ul>
Financial institutions/lenders	<ul><li>Financial strength and stability of the company (for security of the loan).</li><li>Return on investment (e.g., via interest).</li><li>Mutually beneficial ongoing relationship.</li></ul>	<ul><li>Short-term and long-term loan finance to maintain and develop operations.</li><li>Added value services (e.g., insurance, currency management).</li><li>Power to restrict or withdraw credit facilities.</li></ul>

©CIPS 2014

Remember the feeling of being torn between seemingly conflicting interests? This is the group whose needs appear to pull your allegiances in the exact opposite direction from those of the internal stakeholders. Take suppliers, for instance: how often have you found suppliers agreeing with every initiative you introduce? How many times have you had to step in to resolve a dispute between them and your user teams? How many compromises have you had to make back and forth? This relationship degenerates significantly in situations where the user team does not want to work with a certain supplier due to some unfortunate history and bad blood.

This issue is further compounded when the processes and structure have not been firmly set up to ensure transparency and fairness across the board. You will have users complaining about specific supplier performances on the one hand and suppliers grieving about some unfair treatment on the other. Whether these complaints or grievances are fair or not, it is the responsibility of procurement to manage both groups of stakeholders to achieve success; we cannot afford to lose the commitment or trust of either.

We can treat suppliers fairly in the buying process and give them time to prepare and plan for our requirements. We can pay them on time for goods and services delivered and use the supplier relationship model (I will discuss this later) to get people in both organisations talking at the right levels.

External Stakeholders

Table 3

STAKEHOLDER	INTERESTS/NEEDS/ DRIVERS	INFLUENCE/ CONTRIBUTION
Government and regulatory bodies	<ul><li>Corporate tax revenue.</li><li>Healthy level of economic activity.</li><li>Compliance with legislation and regulation.</li><li>Reports and tax returns.</li><li>Support for community development and employment.</li></ul>	<ul><li>Power to enforce requirements through legislation, regulation, penalties.</li><li>Control over tax levels and public funding (e.g., via grants).</li><li>Bargaining power as a large customer or supplier of goods or services.</li><li>Support and guidance for business.</li></ul>
Pressure groups (e.g., Greenpeace), and interest groups (e.g., consumer associations, trade unions)	<ul><li>Promotion and increased awareness of a cause or issue (e.g., fair trade, environment).</li><li>Protection of rights and interests of members.</li><li>Access to information and accountability.</li><li>Sponsorship or donation funding.</li></ul>	<ul><li>May shape policy (e.g., via lobbying).</li><li>Inform and mobilize public and consumer opinion for or against the organisation.</li><li>Source of info regarding issues and impact.</li><li>May collaborate to enhance ethical credentials of the firm or brand.</li><li>Power to mobilize protests or boycotts.</li></ul>
Community and society at large	<ul><li>Access to products and services, employment.</li><li>Product safety.</li><li>Affordability of essential goods and services.</li><li>Socially responsible business and environmental practices: harm minimisation.</li></ul>	<ul><li>Pool of current and potential customers, suppliers, and employees.</li><li>Power to mobilize government policy and consumer opinion.</li></ul>

©CIPS 2014

Our day-to-day interaction with this third group is limited because we do not engage with them regularly. These stakeholders' needs can be met through sheer authority and, sometimes, law, and as such, must be reckoned with in our list of priorities. We must understand the laws affecting our kind of business and design our internal policies to comply with them. We then ensure that we hire good talent from these communities to provide skilled labour and that we implement our corporate social responsibility (CSR) initiatives equitably. Some writers argue that the future of the supply chain is CSV (creating shared value), where corporate organisations partner with the government to execute infrastructure-related projects. This is another way to endear companies to the communities they operate in and add value in the long term.

Organisations as Vehicles: A New Perspective on Business

A few years after I had established myself in the profession, I was reporting to a CEO who wasn't as involved in my role as I wanted him to be. The company was doing quite well, and he had a solid grasp on operations, which is a great quality for CEOs, as a few of them are so far into strategy that they sometimes lose touch with how things really work. Anyway, I didn't feel I was close enough to him as the other executives were, and thus I sensed I was losing the benefits of that relationship. I'm a believer in 'greatness by association', you see, and I stand by the saying, 'If you want to be wise, you need to walk with wise men and women'.

Well, this boss of mine was quite happy with my performance and didn't feel he needed to do anything more to get the best out of me. Every time I walked into his office and wanted to talk about work or other stuff, he would tell me to keep doing what I was doing, that he was really impressed with my team's performance, and that he didn't need to get into the details of procurement. While this might have seemed like a vote of confidence and an excuse to avoid him, I wanted more. In my experience, leaders need to talk to each other often; could this be why your executive team is sometimes in all-day meetings for extended periods? Not all those discussions are comfortable; in fact, some of them are quite difficult to have, especially in times when the business isn't doing so well. People who work together must communicate a lot – good and bad. This is how they get to know and understand each other.

Have you noticed that when you are not performing as expected is when your boss wants to be close to you? That is when he/she starts asking for frequent reports and updates. These people don't like surprises, so they want to know early if something isn't going as planned, so they can report it and take corrective measures.

So, one day, I encountered my CEO in the corridor of his office floor, and I tried to get his attention for an informal session. His answer was the same, all was going fine, and he wasn't worried about anything from my area. At that point, I knew I had to do something desperate, so I asked him this:

'Do you want me to create a problem so it becomes necessary for you to see me?'

It took a few moments for the import of my words to sink in. His countenance dropped as he contemplated the implications of a failing or non-performing procurement department, and then he broke into laughter as he understood it was a plea, couched as a joke, to secure his attention. After he regained his composure, he scheduled a few sessions during which I benefited from his vast experience.

This brings me to an analogy I use quite often. Some have criticised it as not being perfect, but that is not its purpose. I merely use it to drive a point home. It's easier for people to understand something when it's described in terms they identify with.

A procurement/supply chain department is like the engine of a car. You would not need to pop the hood until something goes wrong or when it requires maintenance. It is an important part of the vehicle, but it is a part you almost never have to interact with directly.

When you have a team that delivers in line with set objectives, keeps costs under control, and is well-motivated and engaged, there is a tendency to almost ignore them. 'Why change a winning formula?' The engine, however, is a critical part of a vehicle and plays a massive role in helping the vehicle serve its purpose. My advice to my colleagues who find themselves in the situation I was in is to engage directly and find creative ways to spend time with your company leadership. Take them through your work and listen to their experience and advice. You will learn many things and grow in your career. We want our supply chain teams purring like the high-performance engines that they are.

Since we are talking about cars, I might as well describe other functional parts of an organisation and use that to buttress my point.

I liken sales/customer service to the tires. During an induction exercise for newly joined staff of a company, every department head had to conduct a session on his/her area of the business and take questions from the new employees. This program lasted for about a week, and when it was time for the sales director to speak, he walked in and said, 'This is where the tire meets the road'. I give him credit for this analogy because he is right. The team tasked with direct interaction with external customers and the trade are like the tires of a vehicle that need to be in constant contact with the road surface to create movement.

The external look, shape, and frame of the vehicle would be the public relations/legal department. They carry the responsibility for how the organisation is seen, and they work to make it appeal to the external environment in which it operates.

The brainbox or ECU would be marketing and IT; these functions create the ideas and process the information that is fed to the other functions. Most initiatives begin in marketing, and when there is a change in customer needs, they are tasked to modify the company's product offering.

Human resources would be the lubricant that oils the machine and prevents friction between the parts that rub against each other. HR does a whole lot more, but in terms of core function in this analogy, this is how I define their role.

Finance would be the fuel; they are responsible for ensuring all the adequate finances are available for the organisation to continue its operations efficiently and smoothly.

The executive team is the steering and chassis. They determine the direction of the vehicle and absorb the shock of crashes when they do occur. For newer cars, the steering wheel has command buttons for many of the functions, including the now ubiquitous voice control.

These descriptions are not perfect but just an attempt to create a picture of how different functions work together to achieve the goals of the organisation. For procurement/supply chain, the message is to speak up and not remain in hiding until something goes wrong. Ask to be heard and engage often. This way, you will function optimally and serve your true purpose.

Building and Developing a Procurement Team: Recruitment and Growth Strategies

Many colleagues who find themselves saddled with the responsibility of managing a new team struggle with how to build an organisation and position it to drive results. When you work for a company that has a well-developed supply chain structure, you will typically fit into a well-defined set-up. With small to medium-sized establishments, this is not always the case, and the head of procurement must play a stakeholder influencing role to reach an agreement on what to do. I will explore some possible solutions to this dilemma and provide options to procurement leaders who are dealing with this situation.

My suggestions may also apply to professionals who leave big corporations to take up leadership roles in smaller companies. This is because they may not have been exposed to strategic roles and decision-making opportunities and suddenly find themselves having to wear bigger hats. They need guidance, too, and are a core audience for this material.

You will observe that I have titled the chapter 'Building and Developing a Procurement Team' because you are not always starting from scratch. You will usually be brought in to manage an existing group of professionals with varying levels of capability. These team members will have their own unique experiences and ideas about how things should be done, but most of all, they will be looking to you for leadership and guidance. The decisions you make within a few months of joining will set the tone for your success and make your tenure a fulfilling one.

Procurement Organisation Structure Types

TYPE OF ORGANISATION	DESCRIPTION	PROS	CONS	CENTRAL PROCUREMENT CONTROL	LOCAL P&L RESPONSIBILITY
Decentralised	Procurement takes place in local businesses with no corporate role.	Local control and autonomy embedded in the business. Flat organisation structure with clear accountability. Good match to local supply-based and service.	No volume leverage. No sharing of practices. Duplication of efforts. Reduced ability to invest in people and technology for professionalisation.	Low	High
Centre-led	Small central team for category strategy and supplier segmentation. Local buyers in the business report dotted line into procurement.	Ability to achieve leverage by establishing collaboration across businesses. Limited overhead costs and proximity to the local business maintained. Ability to share best practices and learn from each other.	Requires stronger leadership to ensure local buyers engage. May take longer to professionalise and achieve results. Because businesses can 'opt out', results may only be partially achieved.	Medium	Medium
Centralised	Central procurement organisation for all spend and all buyers report to the procurement function.	Maximum corporate leverage. Easiest to streamline procurement process and develop once for all. Ability to professionalise procurement.	Procurement more removed from the business. Lowered local responsiveness. Risk of overhead and central bureaucracy.	High	Low

Adapted from *Leading Procurement Strategy Driving Value Through the Supply Chain* by Dr Carlos Mena, Remko van Hoek, Martin Christopher 3rd Edition.

Organisation Design Considerations

The assumption is that procurement organisations operate within large corporations with a global presence and therefore have several teams dispersed all over the region with their own reporting lines and strategies serving their business unit. For many small and medium-sized businesses, however, this is not the case. The concept of a decentralised team also means that the procurement function is at an early stage of development and may have any of the below structures:

Reporting directly to the CEO or MD: For many SMEs, the procurement team are mainly fulfilling the order cycle. All decisions are routed through the head of the company, and sometimes, the buying team simply carries out his/her directives. The structure here is not defined as team members assigned tasks as needs arise or based on their demonstrated competency. In some cases, the risk associated with a spend item is the criteria for who is assigned to it. The influence you can exert in such a structure will depend on how much trust you have earned. If, through professionalism and discipline, you can win the confidence of your superiors, you can introduce some order to the team and grow their capability.

Reporting to the CFO/COO/HR director: These organisations are at an early stage in the procurement evolution, except that the CEO chooses to delegate the tasks to a subordinate and merely acts as a final approver. Procurement here is still mainly administrative, with some responsibility for cost savings, which is why supervision is ceded to the CFO.

Head of procurement/supply chain: The models I have experienced here could include a dotted-line reporting structure to the CEO or the factory/plant director. The size of the organisation requires that there is a separate department leadership, but some oversight responsibility is placed on another function.

Reporting line, not location: The differences between the three types of organisational structures reflect differences in reporting lines: to the business, dotted line, or hard line into the function. We must not confuse this with location. In the centralised structure, while buyers all report to a manager within the procurement function, they are not always located in one facility. In fact, it may make sense to locate (some) buyers at the operations facility that own the categories they are responsible for. One of the downsides of this model is that it may defeat the purpose of having a centralised function in the true sense of the word; however, if operational heads feel that their buyers are not close enough to them to understand their needs and best serve their categories, you will need to find a balance that works. In this case, I suggest a solid reporting line to procurement and a dotted line to the operational head. You may also want to schedule job location rotations within the team for such roles that allow different personnel spend time at such facilities and share the responsibility where possible.

Culture is key: On top of the organisational considerations surrounding the organisational structures, do not ignore company culture. If a company is very focused on local decision-making and local operating structures, and the nuances of different regions require an on-the-ground presence, you might want to explore a flexible centralised model. You do not want to put a wedge between procurement and its business partners in the quest to achieve structural ideals.

Don't go against the operating model of the business: This goes without saying. You want your organisational structure to align with the business model. You also want to ensure that your stakeholders are managed satisfactorily. If your setup is not delivering results to the bottom line and not driving stakeholder satisfaction, you might want to review it quickly. Be sure to seek input from more experienced partners within and outside the business.

Whichever structure you choose, be prepared to adapt to business demands over time – as procurement teams mature and businesses and markets change, even the best organisational model may need to be updated.

I have been fortunate to be part of different procurement organisation structures like direct reporting line to the MD/CEO, reporting to the CFO, and reporting to the supply chain director, and I can tell from experience that any one of the above models can work with the strong leadership and team effort.

This decision on what model to operate is a very important decision to make; however, picking the right organisational structure on its own is no guarantee for success. You need to work closely with your stakeholders to deliver on the business results.

Right-Fitting: Choosing the Best Candidates for Your Team

'A leader chooses his/her team'.

Now you have a design that will help you succeed in your role; your next task is to resource or 'right-fit' the organisation. In an earlier chapter, I shared that my first two roles in procurement management offered me an opportunity to choose my team. I had the rare opportunity to restructure the function, evaluate the capabilities of the existing team, make recommendations for who would fit in the new design, and support those who moved on to other departments or companies.

This was a unique situation that most of my readers might not experience. Choosing your team is one of the benefits of leadership. A new CEO chooses his CFO, COO, and other key roles. It is usually a condition for accepting the position in the first place, and you must consider your team to be the most critical to your success. If there are individuals you have worked with or who fit the profile of people who can partner with your vision, you must pursue the prospect of hiring them. The fast-paced corporate environment is no place to give excuses for failure, especially when that shortfall in performance is blamed on a skills gap or poor working relationship with one's team.

If you have the latitude to do so, go ahead and hire members of your team who will lead important categories; this way, you will know that your mission is in the right hands. In this section, I will be describing some typical role profiles/job descriptions that you can use in your hiring process.

Recruiting Experienced Hires

Most managers prefer to hire people who are already working in similar roles so that they can 'hit the ground running'. This is usually the case when there is pressure to deliver or when an employee leaves the team without giving the required notice period. This should not be the case if you have cultivated good working relationships with your staff and you operate an open work culture. I've always said that 'it is the manager's fault if an employee has to hide the fact that he/she is leaving for greener pasture'.

The habit of trying to convince an employee to stay after they have put in a resignation letter is 'medicine after death' at best. Except the employee is seeking to negotiate a salary raise or some other benefit (in which case, they would only use the threat of resignation as a last resort), I consider the feeble attempts to persuade them otherwise as insincere.

How did you ignore them for so long? How come you didn't notice them detaching slowly? When was the last time you had a one-to-one session with them? Did you really care? There is no excuse for losing touch with your direct reports; after all, we are in the business of managing people and not transactions. The time to convince an employee to remain with the organisation and to share your 'big plans' for them is while they are still committed to you. If they have been lured by better opportunities, I suggest you wish them well and let them go.

Some managers tend to create a 'wish list' when developing profiles for the quality of people they seek to fill procurement roles. They include all kinds of capabilities, skills, and years of experience as criteria for the ideal candidate, usually without matching work conditions, compensation, and benefits. The maturity level of the hiring manager and the organisation could be a factor here, but they may struggle to find the right calibre of candidates to respond to such job ads.

A job advert reveals more about the company than you think, and if you could not take the time to draft a job description designed to attract the quality of employee you seek, what does that say about how you treat people?

A typical job advert for an experienced employee should contain the following:

1. Job title as defined in your organogram.
2. Job level (top, middle, or lower-level management) and reporting lines – solid and dotted.
3. An introduction of your organisation and what you are about, with some information on how the role fits into the big picture.
4. The job description in as much detail as possible.
5. Work benefits – health insurance, vehicle, vacations, etc.
6. Salary range – minimum and maximum bands. Why recruiters hesitate to share this critical piece of information remains a mystery.
7. Career path – where progression within the role could lead to in the organisation hierarchy.
8. Direct reports – if any.
9. Key enablers to success – everything provided by the organisation to help the role-holder exceed expectations.
10. Possible roadblocks to optimal performance – are there qualities that may hinder accomplishment in the role, for instance, an inability to effectively manage a diverse stakeholder community?
11. Any policies on remote working and how that affects the position.
12. Travel requirements and percentage of work time spent outside of the office.

Experienced candidates are probably working elsewhere, and if they are good performers, their managers will want to keep them. The job market is competitive, and other companies will attract the same people you are targeting. The more information they find in a job ad helps them reach decisions quicker. Now, if withholding any of the above information helps you secure top-quality candidates, please go ahead, and make that argument.

The hiring manager must be fully involved in the process and should not just delegate to HR. Your human resources department is the custodian of the recruitment exercise and will provide the guardrails so people adhere to company policy. They are not experts at identifying and nurturing top talent within our profession. The people they eventually hire will be working directly with you, and you should care that you are getting the right employees through the activity.

Now, this is not to degrade the excellent work our colleagues in HR are doing, but when you really think about it, many in their positions are also young and may not have the experience required to sort through the clutter and help you find capable people. Some of them, to their credit, are more focused on the process than the outcome. The hiring manager is most qualified to manage this exercise and should make time to lead it with the support of HR.

With the interview process itself, I propose the following approach:

Screening

If you have a comprehensive job description with clearly defined criteria for the ideal candidate you are hoping to hire, the screening process will be easy to get through. Whether you are using an ATS (applicant tracking system) or not, certain highlighted qualities will 'jump' out at you from the submitted resumes. Be sure to look out for real work experience, and don't be misled by candidates who 'game' the ATS by using relevant keywords.

Aptitude Tests/Skills Assessment

I strongly recommend aptitude tests as a screening method for low to mid-level roles. This job requires a good grasp of basic math and oral/written verbal reasoning skills. You don't want to spend your time dealing with people who struggle with simple calculations or who turn you into a Microsoft spell checker when they send documents for review or approval. There are many platforms that organise these as procurement/supply chain skills assessment exams or MCQs on general knowledge and computer skills. Subscribe to one of these if you do not have the time to develop an assessment yourself. The costs are reasonable, and you can use them on a one-off basis only when you need to do a recruitment exercise.

Assessment Centres/Case Studies

An assessment centre is an all-day session where you bring all the shortlisted candidates and interviewers together to get to know one another in an atmosphere where you can observe candidates interact with each other and show their capability. A typical assessment would include:

Introduction/Icebreaker

After sharing the agenda and guidelines for the session, the candidates would sit around a conference table and introduce themselves. Questions such as 'What animal best describes you?' 'What kind of work environment or culture would encourage your best self to emerge?' etc. These questions are meant to help the candidates relax, loosen up, and prepare for the day. There are no scores for this, just an opportunity to hear them express themselves.

Group Exercise

This is the first time the candidates would have to work together, and a great opportunity for interviewers to observe the dynamics of the group and how individuals interact with their peers. The facilitator would share details of an exercise on the screen and ask the team to study it and make a presentation to the interviewing panel after a set time limit. Typically, there are no instructions for the group, and they are expected to decide how best to approach the exercise among themselves. Scores are given to people who take on the role of scribe/secretary, records/note-taker, timekeeper, moderator (organiser), lead presenter, support lead presenter, strong knowledge contributors, and other roles that they create as they work together. The objective here is to identify people who embrace their roles and do their utmost to contribute positively. The brilliance of their contribution will not necessarily be a basis for a low or high score. Are they willing to come out of their shell and engage with others? The work environment will require constant and proactive interaction, and the candidates should try to work with others, regardless of how they feel about themselves or each other. The final score for the presentation outcome will be awarded equally among all participants regardless of who makes the presentation.

Case Study

This is the first real evaluation of the candidates' individual capability on the day. They will be expected to review a comprehensive case study – usually a challenge your organisation is dealing with or has dealt with – and provide professional proposals for addressing them. They will be expected to use procurement models, principles, their experience, and industry knowledge. Ideally, this example and the solutions they offer have to be in line with the kind of work they will be doing:

1. Category managers should develop a simple sourcing strategy or the outline of one.
2. Lower-level managers should tackle a supplier performance challenge or a complex expediting process with a difficult stakeholder.
3. Other case study topics could relate to policy issues, stakeholder management, or other examples from the day-to-day job of the role holder.

Some organisations issue the case study context a few days before the assessment centre and allow the candidates to take their time to talk through their proposals with the panel. I identify with this because it best simulates the work environment.

Candidates are allowed to use every available source of information as reference and should not be restricted from using their resources to get relevant data. Asking them to work on memory alone will not be representative of the typical work at the office and may put undue pressure on the candidates, and that is not the objective of the activity.

Another advantage of receiving their presentations early is that the hiring manager and interviewers would have had time to go through and prepare questions to test the candidate's knowledge to separate those who know their stuff from those who simply copy off the internet or someone else.

One-On-One Oral Interview

Here, the standard behavioural question and answer session is expected, with ample time for documenting answers and scoring. Answers should be probed until all relevant information has been obtained and the candidate's questions answered. This may be conducted as a separate activity or, if you are unable to convene the interview panel for another session, as part of the assessment centre.

Scoring

All panellists will score and calibrate at the end of the day so a decision can be reached and offers considered. Calibration is required so you do not end up with scores that vary too much from the general perception of the candidates. I advise that the decision is made on the same day and, in the case where two candidates are neck and neck, a chat with the hiring manager should be scheduled for not more than a week after the session. This chat is merely a formality and helps the manager choose between two top contenders.

Resumption and Settling In

Recruiting is time-consuming, and you should make the time to do it right, or you will be stuck with people who either don't fit in with your culture or who you will have to micro-manage to get value out of the relationship. If you thought the hard work was over, think again. The induction of transition from new hire to productive employee is the most critical part of the process. The new employee's experience on their first day, week, or month can set the tone for their behaviour and performance for the rest of their tenure.

Again, it is the responsibility of the hiring manager supported by HR to give the new employee an experience that will make them want to give their best at work. I believe that the decision to stay with an organisation is made within the first few days of resumption. Aside from all the company setup and relocation issues (if the candidate is moving in from elsewhere), I think that the most important part of settling in will have to do with the work they were hired for. I mentioned earlier that I give new employees (entry-level) two to three months and one month for experienced hires to settle in. During this time, I avoid giving them work to do, and now I will share the activity plan I use for this period.

- Week 1 – Company introductions, office/IT setup (desk space, emails, phones, access to server data), office tour, studying company HR policies, and other important guidelines.

- Week 2 – Our procurement principles and how we work, including examples of reports, work documents, approval documents, templates, procurement policies, SOPs, and other relevant materials.

- Week 3 – Stakeholder introductions and meetings with colleagues from other units to review expectations, discuss work plans, and agree on ways of working.

- Week 4 – Supplier visits (which should have been scheduled in advance) to understand their operations and how they interface with our organisation.

Every week, the manager will have a personal review with them to test what they've learnt, check in on how they're doing, and provide answers to any questions they might have.

After the above, I expect them to start work in earnest.

Head of Procurement Focus Areas: Leading the Team to Success

I have often been asked for a list of activities for a newly appointed head of procurement. What should the person be focused on? This question usually comes from people who did not work under an experienced supervisor or from those who were fortunate to secure the role from a junior position. I have created these steps from my experience, and they can be changed to suit the role in question. What I have found, however, is that when you systematically approach your work this way, you lay a strong foundation for your future success.

If you have just been promoted to the role of head of procurement, category buyer, senior buyer, or any role that gives you responsibility within procurement, and you have been at a loss for how to excel in that position, consider the suggestions below.

1. PUT TOGETHER THE RIGHT TEAM – Whether you're hiring or restructuring, be sure to have the right team working with you. You will only deliver results that are as good as your team, so do not compromise on this one. You will find a lot of guidance in this book, and I encourage you to use it. If you do nothing else, do everything to have a strong team supporting you in your role.

2. DEVELOP CORE PROCUREMENT SKILLS – This applies to you and your team. Do not be ashamed to learn stuff you do not know, and make it a priority to expose yourself and your team to the best training available. Even when people assume that you know everything, do not agree with their opinion. Ask for help from people who know better; you will be better off when you do.

3. GOVERNANCE/AUDIT READINESS – Review your SOPs and governance documentation thoroughly. You will quickly lose credibility if an audit throws up red flags and indicates that your

department is a risk to the organisation. This is one area you cannot delegate; own this and set the tone for compliance in your organisation.

4. TRUST YOUR TEAM/COLLEAGUES TO DELIVER – If you have provided the relevant development tools for your team, please step back and let them work. Hovering over and micro-managing them leaves them wondering if you trust them. Review their work periodically and ensure that they are getting the help they need to deliver, then let them take the credit when it's deserved. When they fail or make mistakes, deal with it privately and defend them publicly; always make it clear that you are on their side.

5. KPIS/PERFORMANCE MEASUREMENT – Agree on SLAs with your stakeholders and the criteria for performance measurement. Do not leave this to their whims at appraisal time. Track and report result monthly such that you will simply be aggregating at the end of the fiscal year. User departments are often subjective when they fill out customer satisfaction survey forms and may sometimes score you and your team based on certain standout incidents that stick in their memory. If you score monthly or quarterly, you will have a more objective basis to assess overall performance.

6. DETERMINE BUSINESS REQUIREMENTS – Do this by using spend analysis data, budgets, and attending business strategy meetings. Review previous spend data, ensure you are included in on budgets and plans, and request invitations to key meetings. If you are constantly surprised by purchase requests from your internal stakeholders, you will never stay ahead of the issues. There will be the odd emergency every now and then or needs triggered by a change in markets, and this is okay; just don't spend your career fighting fires.

7. STAKEHOLDER ENGAGEMENT – Meet with your stakeholders monthly to review work progress, discuss upcoming projects, and find time to have informal outings. Build strong relationships that will make them allies. Work relationships are strengthened by out-of-work interaction. Attend their events, invite them to yours, go for lunches,

dinners, and play some sports together if your interests align. Use those moments to learn more about each other; you will reap the rewards when you get back to work and need to rely on one another for some deliverable.

8. UNDERSTAND VALUE FROM YOUR STAKEHOLDERS' PERSPECTIVE – While developing these relationships, be clear with stakeholders about what they see as value. What does success look like from their perspective? Discuss and agree on these, then work to deliver. You, alone, cannot determine value: the recipient is better suited to define what solutions best meet their needs. Just like customers' needs guide a company's product/service offerings, our user departments are best positioned to tell us what they want. Yes, some compromises need to be made, and this is okay; just don't go off doing your own thing and expect that they will appreciate your efforts.

9. ALIGN ON IMPLEMENTATION PLANS – For every project, be sure to seek and gain their contribution. Define your and their teams' input and ask for their support when needed. When you are working on a project, share your schedule and build their deadlines into your critical path. Be cognizant of their priorities and ways of working and adjust to accommodate changes in their program where required.

10. REVIEW AND REPORT PROGRESS – Design periodic reports to track your teams' progress and develop cross-functional reports that you can review with your stakeholders so you do not have surprises at the end of the year. Report, report, report. As the saying goes…

> *'Overcommunicate. It's better to tell someone something they already know than to not tell them something they needed to hear'.*
>
> — *Alex Irvine, Pacific Rim: The Official Movie Novelization*

Growth and Development: Nurturing Your Procurement Team

When something stops growing, it becomes a fossil.

Therefore, the manager of procurement professionals should have a plan to constantly grow the knowledge and capability of his/her team. Career growth is the responsibility of the individual, period. However, the manager has a duty to provide the enablers for said growth to occur. This includes identifying and advertising courses, leaders, and these days, social media handles of good quality content that his/her team would attend and follow, giving them time off for study and exams, and making full use of the L&D (learning and development) budget.

When L&D is kicked down the road (until quarter 4, for instance, when it is done to tick the box), the options of trainers, facilitators, and venues available are not always of the best quality. We do not want to be counted among those who do training just because HR needs to meet its KPI. The dynamic nature of the profession requires that our knowledge be updated on the go. As companies innovate and lead with new ways to solve problems, we should stay aware and find ways to link those solutions to our company's needs.

Some organisations use a competency framework, where the acquisition of certain skills is linked to training received and projects done. This competency framework would have skill levels – beginner, advanced, and expert – where delivery against specific projects is required to assess and score individuals. Managing a competency framework in this manner provides a clear career progression path for procurement professionals and makes employee performance discussions issue-based vs. the subjective approach many of us take today.

If you look at your procurement team, can you honestly say that you have a well-defined career path from entry-level to head of procurement? Do your team members know for certain what level of performance they need to put in to move from one level to the next? Is this documented and signed on by the business leadership? Does your team have testimonials of people who have benefited from this scheme, if you have one, or is it just on paper?

Let us look at some examples you might want to adopt and customise for your use:

Level	Competitive Bidding Skills and Knowledge
BEGINNER	Understands basic concepts and terminology of competitive bidding. Can identify and evaluate potential bid opportunities. Can develop and initiate a basic RFx package.
ADVANCED	Has demonstrated BEGINNER skills in addition to: Has a solid understanding of the competitive bidding process. Can prepare and issue RFx documents and evaluation criteria. Can identify and mitigate risks associated with an RFx. Can develop and conduct an RFx that drive and achieves value for the business.
EXPERT	Has demonstrated ADVANCED skills in addition to: Has a thorough understanding of the competitive bidding process and can apply it in complex and high-stakes projects. Can anticipate and respond to changes in the competitive landscape. Can lead a diverse team through the RFx process and manage relationships with key stakeholders. Has a deep understanding of market trends and can identify and pursue innovation opportunities. Has a strong track record of successful RFx projects and delivering value. Has extensive knowledge of legal and regulatory requirements related to bidding and contract award. Can develop and implement effective RFx strategies. Can analyse and interpret financial data and make informed decisions. Has strong communication and negotiation skills. Has a deep understanding of the industry and can anticipate and respond to changes in technology and market trends.

Level	Negotiation Skills and Knowledge
BEGINNER	Understands basic concepts and terminology of negotiations. Can identify and evaluate potential negotiation opportunities. Can prepare for and conduct simple negotiations. Understands the basics of the negotiation process.
ADVANCED	Has demonstrated BEGINNER skills in addition to: Has a solid understanding of the negotiation process. Can detect and take advantage of negotiation opportunities. Can identify and mitigate risks associated with negotiations. Can develop and lead a successful negotiation process. Understands negotiation and contract management best practices. Can apply different negotiation styles, techniques, and strategies.
EXPERT	Has demonstrated ADVANCED skills in addition to: Has a thorough understanding of the negotiation process and can apply it in complex and high-stakes situations. Can anticipate and respond to changes in difficult supplier negotiations. Can lead a team through a complex negotiation process and manage relationships with key stakeholders. Has a deep understanding of market trends and opportunities and can identify and pursue alternatives. Has a strong track record of successful negotiations. Has strong communication skills. Understands and can apply advanced negotiation techniques and strategies like BATNA, ZOPA, and interest-based negotiation.

Level	Sourcing Strategy Skills and Knowledge
BEGINNER	Translates business unit needs into relevant long and short-term goals. Develops tactical plans, executes, and renews them, keeping supplier relationships in mind. Uses SWOT analysis to identify strategic themes from the data and create strategies. Uses Industry and Supplier analysis skills in the development and execution of the strategy. Appropriately differentiates between strategic and tactical sourcing; ensures that high impact items get maximum effort by setting priorities and focusing strategies. Balances short and long-term needs by delivering results. Balances the need to maintain the strategic course (despite day-to-day variation and pressures) with the need to change the strategy if fundamental conditions change. Knows the thought process for developing sourcing strategies and pragmatically applies it.
ADVANCED	Has demonstrated BEGINNER skills in addition to: Integrates the formulation of sourcing strategies with other functional strategies in the business by proactively ensuring that procurement perspective is considered and incorporated in the development of such strategies. Has successfully led the development of complex sourcing strategies in challenging situations that delivered key results. Uses experience and knowledge of which sourcing strategies work (or not) and why they work, as a basis for continual improvement and reapplication. Trains others on sourcing strategies Able to influence the material market through strategies and tactics to deliver competitive advantage to the company across multiple goods and services.
EXPERT	Has demonstrated ADVANCED skills plus the following: Is widely and consistently recognised as a thought leader on sourcing strategies. Proactively ensures that global strategic considerations are reflected in major sourcing decisions, provides oversight to avoid outages/misses on such issues. Has progressed beyond just developing strategies to improving the sourcing strategy process. Influences the formulation of company business strategies by proactively ensuring that procurement knowledge and perspective are considered early and incorporated in the development of such strategies.

These do not constitute a comprehensive list of skills or competencies, but it shows that it is possible to have a framework across different skills.

In addition to the above examples, the individual would have worked on specific projects that validate the use and mastery of this skill at the different levels to be certified and will benefit from the career rewards that come with it. The recommended approach is to have the individual submit work that demonstrates these skills and sit with an expert (line manager or consultant) to validate the said skill.

This process is how I got certified in procurement skills across different competencies, and I recommend it confidently.

Next, we will be looking at standard operating procedure (SOP) guidelines for procurement.

Procurement Policies and SOP Elements: Creating Guidelines for Best Practices

The Authority of a Comprehensive Procurement Policy

In every organisation, there are policies (written or unwritten) that guide decision-making. From multipage folders – sometimes automated – to the thoughts and whims of the boss, these policies are the guidelines for employee and department activities within the company.

For those people who say that their organisations don't have any, I will only ask you to observe patiently until you or someone else does something to disrupt operations; you will (very quickly) become aware of these policies!

Now, policies are guidelines for action set up by government and non-government organisations that define the way they want companies to work. Policies are like big signboards that say, 'Look out, this is how we want you to do things!' They inform insiders and outsiders of what is allowed and, more importantly, what is not allowed within that sphere of operations. In fact, one of the reasons they say African businesses don't outlive their founders is because of the absence of enduring business policies.

With procurement, this becomes even more critical, as for most companies, the procurement department is the major funnel through which money goes out. If the main avenue through which resources are expended doesn't have strong guidelines, there is a risk that such an organisation will not remain in business for very long.

I will now address two major benefits of having a good procurement policy in your organisation.

The first is **control** – a comprehensive procurement policy gives you control of your operations and puts you in charge of your work. This means that you get to write your own manual. A lot of work in procurement has to do with managing exceptions. You have a process for getting things done, but your boss or an important stakeholder wants it done a different way. With a well-written policy, you can capture typical exceptions and how they should be handled, who requests them, and who approves them. Learning this early in my procurement career completely changed the way I managed expectations. Don't sit down frustrated and feel like a victim under the pressure of so many non-compliant requests; build those exceptions into your policy and take control!

The second is **audits** – internal and external auditors are the bane of procurement organisations. No matter how hard you've worked through the year, a poor audit report can make you feel completely helpless. These auditors can find snow in a desert! They seem to target the only transactions you failed to normalise, and they end up making a big deal out of those. However, if you recognise that they are only doing their jobs and that audits will never go away, you can learn to embrace them and work with them to improve your processes. Use the feedback from the auditors to strengthen the weak areas of your policy documents and include a process for self-reporting violations. You must also note that an auditor will only evaluate your work based on the policy documents you have, and this further builds on my case for a well-written, comprehensive policy document!

Contents of a Good Procurement Policy

There are different standards for what the sections of a procurement policy should contain. My suggestions below are guidelines that attempt to cover a few of the most important elements. If the procedures in your organisation require much more than these, please proceed to include them as required.

Responsibilities

A good procurement policy should define the roles and approval levels of the key players in an organisation who are involved in the procurement process. From the board of directors down to the requester, every approving authority and user of the policy should be listed (by role and not by name), and their duties regarding the procurement process should be mentioned. From setting up the policy document itself to price forecasts, budgets, and cost-saving targets to how the supplier database should be managed, when and how to evaluate supplier performance, to which documents should be preserved for audit purposes and for how long. There must be no ambiguity with regard to who should be responsible for certain processes and the level of authority that person has within the process. This is the first step to having a process that is inclusive and helps everyone in the organisation know and play their part without fear of violating the policy.

Procurement Standards

In every organisation, there are standards for everything. These refer to the minimum criteria that must be met for decisions to be made. Buying decisions are quite critical to the survival and growth of companies, and because procurement is the main (if not only) pipe through which money flows out of an organisation, it becomes imperative that the rules for spending such money are laid out somewhere.

For instance:

- What is in scope of the procedure document and what is not?
- What is the requisition (RFx) process? How should requisitioners buy stuff? What process should they follow?
- When and for what amount of spend should a purchase order be required?
- When do you need a contract? Who should approve contracts?
- What are the conditions for any of the above to be carried out?
- Are there other policies linked to these that need to be consulted for clarity?

- Where are these other policies located?

Now you may think that your organisation is too small or that decisions are made at the whim of your boss, but what if you drafted a document detailing these criteria and showed it to your boss for their review and approval? What if this document showed him/her how your organisation could be more audit compliant and how it would make your processes up to date and how it could only be updated and approved with their input? Any good boss would want that and will reward such an employee. Of course, these procedures are more mandatory for companies that are listed on the stock exchange, but small companies grow, and my suggestions are for procurement people who want to develop themselves and take their careers into their own hands.

Self-Audit Principle

This section is missing from most procurement policies because very few people recognise its importance or even consider its existence. Just like most modern urinals have an automated flush system that releases water into the bowl every few minutes (even without being used), it is standard practice for procurement policies to contain self-audit requirements and processes that allow them to run violation reports and sense check those same guidelines periodically.

The perception of the procurement function is only further clouded by damaging audit reports. These reports come as a shock to the business and give the impression that someone has been caught doing something wrong. Now, what if you could have 'arrested' yourself and fixed the issues long before the audit? There is a verse in the Holy Scriptures that says, 'make peace with your adversary while you are on your way to court'. This puts further emphasis on doing self-checks and course corrections long before an audit is conducted.

Every good procurement policy should contain a procedure for self-audits, and procurement leaders must have a process for conducting these periodically. Possible violations are detected early, and updates are made to the policy to prevent future incidents or to redesign defective procedures.

Document Retention

Procurement documents contain commercial transactions but are also legal in nature. Purchase orders, terms and conditions, contracts, non-disclosure agreements, memoranda of understanding, letters of intent, etc. When there are disputes over the fulfilment of obligations, these documents are used for reference by courts and investigating bodies to determine what rights pertain to either party or to prove that the correct processes were followed in reaching a decision. It is always embarrassing to senior management when procurement teams cannot produce such documents or spend loads of time searching through disorganised computer folders and physical cabinets.

Twice in my career, I have had to pull out documents from my personal archives in response to an enquiry that had legal implications. A few months after I had resigned from a previous company, I got a call regarding a transaction that I had managed while I was there. As part of my handover tasks, I had ensured that all hard and soft copies of transactions were in the care of my successor. Unfortunately, he also left the organisation, and this created a gap. When I got the call asking if I had copies of these documents, I simply accessed my archived folders and sent the files to my former boss.

The lesson here is this: every procurement policy must have clear guidelines for document retention.

What documents should be retained? Where/how should they be stored? How long should they be in storage? Some organisations go as far as storing sensitive documents at an off-site location. This is done as part of a business continuity plan and ensures that such documents can be retrieved if the office premises are affected by some unforeseen disaster.

Under the Nigerian Data Protection Law, certain transaction records are required to be stored for up to 10 years, and in the case of police incident reports, permanently. Now you see why this is not just a policy decision; it's a matter that has legal implications.

Separation of Duties

A good procurement policy should contain clear guidelines for the separation of duties. A simple way to do this would be to have a matrix that describes the steps in the procurement process and the responsible authority for that process. For example, the authority or person who makes the requisition should not be the same person who approves the order. In case the reason for this is lost on you, if the same person can raise a request and approve the purchase, it exposes the company to significant risk. This means that certain purchases can be initiated and executed within one role! There are exceptions to this, of course, but my message is clear. Any auditor worth his salt will flag such a process as a risk and will require a compensating control to protect the organisation.

The separation of duties element is easily missed by most organisations because of limitations in staffing or because the CEO always signs off on significant purchases. This is an accident waiting to happen, however, and must be considered to protect the company from a major risk.

Conflict of Interest

The conflict-of-interest principle is well understood in the private and public sectors because it applies in many other areas of work outside procurement. It is, in essence, the existence of any factor or factors that influence the process under consideration. A conflict-of-interest declaration with appropriate approvals MUST be signed off by parties involved in any aspect of the procurement process – from requisition to approval, goods receipt, and vendor payment. Any of these roles can be conflicted in the process and make decisions that benefit them instead of the company. While it is true that the HR department usually requests an annual acknowledgement of a company-wide conflict of interest declaration, the procurement organisation should follow up with a transaction-based declaration. This declaration will cover individuals within the process who have 'conflicts' and wish to announce them upfront so that critical parts of the procurement process will not be assigned to them.

Examples of conflicts of interest in the procurement process:

- A requisitioner may indicate a preference for a single source transaction because of close ties to that vendor.
- A procurement buyer may own shares in specific companies that constantly bid for business.
- A purchase order approver may accelerate certain POs because of promises of settlement.
- A good receiver at the warehouse may overlook defects and shortages in deliveries if he is promised a reward.
- An accounts payable staff may provide justification for expedited payment to a vendor with whom he/she is related.

The transaction-based conflict of interest declaration may not avert these fraudulent activities outright, but it gives the organisation some cover when such activities are reported and exposed.

These sections of a procurement policy provide an excellent foundation for the rest of the content and will be a solid addition to your procedures if you don't already have them.

Developing a Map of the Procurement Process

In designing guidelines for a procurement function, this is probably the heart of the matter. What exactly is the process to be followed when user departments need to issue requests? As basic as some of these things seem, you will find that many organisations do not define them clearly, thus leaving room for misunderstanding and ambiguity in the process.

When I join a procurement organisation, one of the first things I like to do is to review the policy to ensure that it conforms to 'best practices' and then organise roadshows across every user department where I explain the policy (including the purchasing process) and take suggestions from these stakeholders on how we can best work together. It is unfortunate that some procurement processes remain shrouded in mystery and departments who require our services are made to grope around in a minefield trying to avoid being caught in a violation.

How many of you have been caught by a traffic sign you did not see? You know those spots where law enforcement officers suddenly appear out of nowhere and 'confront' you for a violation you didn't even know you committed? How did it make you feel? This is what our stakeholders experience when we do not clearly document our processes and share them with them. Every unit within the company should participate in these 'procurement process roadshows' and should have access to updated copies of our policy and guidelines, including references, templates, and toolkits; these should all be stored on a shared drive, preferably.

The purchasing process is a workflow of tasks and dependencies to be followed when engaging with the procurement department. Timelines and responsibilities for each task should be agreed upon and detailed for everyone to understand and comply with. Everything that needs to happen from when a need is created up until a vendor is paid and evaluated should be documented and laid out like a map. People who interact with procurement need to know where to go and how to get there.

You should also list the types of requests your organisation sends to procurement. You cannot treat every request in the same way. If you have a process that restricts you to competitive bids for every transaction. for instance, you will struggle with requests for OEM equipment, housing, or warehouses. Itemise every type of request you have received and put them in categories. Determine the most effective way to handle these requests and document a process that drives value for your company. Include this in your policy document, seek alignment with your stakeholders, and get it signed off.

There are many sources you could reference for sample documents: the CIPS website (www.cips.org) is a great place to start. Members can find a lot of helpful documents that can be customised to suit their needs. You can also engage the services of an experienced consultant to help optimise your internal processes.

If you keep procurement principles and ethics at the core of your operation, you can be flexible with the methods you use. The objective is to deliver value within the framework of best practices and global standards. Do not attempt to participate in a boxing match with your hands tied behind your back.

Dealing with Exceptions to the Procurement Process

The problem with rules is that people like to test the limits of how far they can go. Most rules have loopholes that will be exploited by creative individuals, so if you spend your time chasing every offender, you will have your hands full trying to ensure adherence. You will then become a police officer instead of a business leader, and that, my friends, is a distraction from what we are called to do.

I'm often asked this question, 'What do you think about managing non-compliance and managing people who violate processes?' This is my usual answer: 'When you have an infestation of pests inside a room, how do you proceed to eliminate the problem? Do you throw stones and objects at them and bring in more furniture, hoping you will crush them by the sheer weight of these items, or do you empty the room one object at a time until they have nowhere to hide?' As you make more rules hoping to 'catch' violators in their game, the more inventive they become in finding ways to evade those procedures.

I propose a different approach; write those exceptions into the procurement process. Business operations are dynamic, and you really cannot account for everything that may occur, so do a historical analysis of the usual exceptions, create a process for getting them approved (usually at the highest level), and include them in the procedure document. This process must include the reason for the exception and be signed off by the highest authority within their department.

You must realise that I am, in essence, asking you to write a 'rule for the exception'. I know that exceptions will occur, and I know that user departments will find a way to fulfil the needs of the business if they make a strong enough case. Business needs will always rank above the procurement processes when push comes to shove.

People usually come back at me with, 'Why are you showing them how to avoid the process and giving them a way out?' Well, I'm not. First, they already know how to navigate their way around the rules, so there's no need to pretend it's not already happening. Secondly, I'm only 'clearing the room' so I can see more clearly why they make these exceptions. It is only when the reasons for the exceptions are known that I can define a process that better manages it.

In my experience, I have seen that business leaders can approve an exception only a few times before they begin to question why their people are not complying. If you keep a record of the number of times each leader has had to approve an exemption and you report it periodically, those same business leaders will begin to push back at their own people and will ask them to work within the framework of the procurement process. All the excuses of procurement being a bottleneck become baseless, and the real problem – a lack of adequate planning by the users – comes to the fore.

This does not mean that procurement people are always in the right, but it provides some insight into what the issues are and how we can partner with our users to provide solutions that drive value and meet the business need at the same time.

Procurement Standard Operating Process (Sop) Guideline Sections

When preparing an SOP for your department, these are section headers you might include:

1. Document Approval
2. Distribution List
3. Approach to Procurement
4. Core Values
5. Introduction
6. Objectives
7. Procurement Strategy
8. Areas of Responsibility
9. Compliance & Governance
10. Code of Conduct
11. Separation/Segregation of Duties Matrix
12. Exclusions to the Policy
13. Conflict of Interest
14. Ethical Procurement Guidelines
15. Sustainability requirements
16. Procurement Process Overview
17. Procurement Process Policies & Procedures
    i. Purchase Requisition Creation (PR)
    ii. Purchase Requisition Approval process
    iii. Special Purchase Requests - Emergency Purchase Request, Urgent Purchase Requests, After the Fact Purchase Requests, Direct Purchase Request (e.g., OEM),

Rental/Lease Purchase Requests, External Repairs Purchase Requests, Budgetary Requests, etc.

    iv. Department Contacts

    v. Communications & Meetings with Suppliers

    vi. Purchasing Exception List

18. Sourcing Standards & Principles

    i. Tender/Inquiry Process

    ii. Inquiry Process Standards & Principles

    iii. Types of Enquiries - Open Bidding, Closed Bidding, etc.

19. Commercial Agreement/Contract criteria

    i. Goods/Services Receipts procedure

    ii. Invoice Verification Process

    iii. Advances/Down Payment

    iv. Credit Claims

    v. Cash Payments

    vi. Sales & Auctions

20. Procurement Controlling Reports

21. Supplier Management

    i. Overview

    ii. Scope

    iii. Pre-Qualification

    iv. Process

    v. Supplier Relationship Management process

    vi. Supplier Relationship Management Matrix

    vii. Krailjc Matric and the Portfolio Model

    viii. Supplier Classification

    ix. Supplier Engagement Model

    x. Supplier Performance Management and Evaluation Process

    xi. Non-Disclosure and Confidentiality

22. Audits

    i. Procurement Documentation Requirements

    ii. Document Retention

    iii. Non-Compliance with Policy

    iv. Legal Requirements

Suppliers' Information Booklet

In addition to the procurement process guideline document, I propose an information booklet for your vendors. If your company has a supplier portal, then this serves the same purpose. It is an onboarding plan like you have for new employees, and it would contain all the details they need to know when engaging with your company.

A suppliers' information booklet is a document that contains information about a company's suppliers, their products and services, and the company's policies and procedures related to working with suppliers. The contents of a suppliers' information booklet would include:

- A signed non-disclosure agreement that commits the vendors to guard company information and to treat it with confidentiality.

- A signed code of conduct detailing the company's policy towards vendors and relationships with members of staff.

- The requirements for vendor registration with details of relevant contacts.

- Purchase order process, including information on orders are placed with suppliers and guidelines to follow when working on such orders.

- Payment terms, including information on how suppliers will be paid, including invoicing procedures and payment schedules.

- Quality control standards, including information on the company's quality control standards and how suppliers are expected to meet them.

- Delivery and logistics, including information on how products and services will be delivered to the company, including any specific requirements or guidelines.

- Compliance and regulations, including information on any legal or regulatory compliance requirements that suppliers need to be aware of when working with the company.

- Communication and feedback, including information on how suppliers can communicate with the company and provide feedback on their services.

- Additional resources, including invoice templates, the process for receiving deliveries and services, the payment process and other resources that can help suppliers work effectively with the company.

Procurement Objectives: The 6 Rights for Successful Procurement

'To the unskilled procurement employee, any reduction in a quoted price is seen as value'.

When I think of the multifaceted stakeholder relationships a procurement professional must manage effectively to be regarded as a success on the job, the image that forms in my mind is that of a juggler. The skills required of such a performer are that he/she must always have some balls in their hands and some in the air. To catch a ball, you must toss another one and deftly repeat this manoeuvre consistently with both hands! A good juggler never 'drops the ball'. This is the case with procurement. There are mainly six imperatives we are tasked with: PRICE, QUALITY, QUANTITY, PLACE, TIME, AND SOURCE.

The ideal transaction is one where all these balls are controlled expertly in the air, but this is not always the case. You may not deliver the optimal target for every transaction or project (though that is the objective), but you will at least be aware of which ones suffer in your attempt to drive value. You will also engage your stakeholders knowledgeably and inform them of the risks/benefits of pushing certain targets.

RIGHT PRICE

To accurately determine the right price, we need to understand the cost structure. What are the cost elements of the supplier's price? What factors influence those costs, and how many of those factors are under their control? The industry analysis tool is one way to gain insight into supplier cost drivers.

Then we must do detailed calculations on life cycle costs or total cost of ownership (TCO). Acquisition costs (initial costs, transport costs, installation/commissioning costs, initial cost of spares, training costs); operation and maintenance costs (supervision, operator wages/salaries, energy costs, cost of materials used, insurance, servicing costs, wear and tear of spares, storage costs, maintenance of materials, depreciation); and lastly, disposal costs (including environmental impact and sustainability requirements). Where required, we might need to show the opportunity costs of not choosing any of the other alternatives.

The price at which an item is procured is important because it is quite visible at the point of purchase, but hidden costs can negate all your hard work if you do not consider them in your evaluation of value. Value is often arrived at through collaborative exercises with your stakeholders. Procurement cannot define value exclusively. If your internal customer places other business priorities above price, you must pull other levers in that transaction to deliver value.

Savings has always been the standard by which procurement performance is measured; however, an ability to manage all the imperatives mentioned in the first paragraph (juggling the balls) will ensure that your outcome will be satisfactory. Using the correct parameters, a financial value can be derived for each element of the 6 procurement imperatives of quality, quantity, source/supplier, price, place, and time. If you can develop a balanced scorecard that attributes a figure to each one of these elements, you will have some positive results to show in your annual performance evaluation.

I remember having a discussion with my supply chain director in one of my previous roles, and he asked me if I thought procurement was a cost centre or a profit centre. My answer was as follows: Tell me what you consider as 'VALUE' to you, and I will deliver on that. In other words, don't pay me a salary or a bonus until I have 'saved' the money/value you are to reward me with.

Value must be defined in collaboration with your stakeholders. Do not sit down and pressure yourself to deliver 'savings' when that is not what your stakeholders want. Focus on value and ensure that your impact is felt across the organisation. You will be better recognised as a valuable business partner, and your influence will grow if you adopt this approach.

At first glance, these objectives appear uncomplicated and easy to attain. In a live scenario, however, you will appreciate the difficulty of meeting every one of these requirements to the level of satisfaction your stakeholders expect. This is because one target is usually compromised so the others can be achieved. There is no such thing as a 'perfect procurement request'. If you had all the money to pay for the right quality and quantity of a needed item/service from your supplier of choice, you obviously don't have all the time you need to secure it or all the space to store it in your preferred location. These 'balls' are moving targets and, as such, must be balanced to the extent that the circumstances allow. I will address them one by one.

QUALITY

Asking some user departments to clearly 'spec' their requests is an ongoing battle. They usually either insist on top-quality brands (which cost way more than the business can afford), or they send unclear parameters, which put procurement in a ping-pong match with suppliers seeking clarity. Some ill-intentioned users go as far as using a specific supplier's design in their requests which makes it impossible for other vendors to quote correctly. My recommendation is for user departments to define the outcome they desire; this will allow some flexibility with determining which solution best meets those needs.

Quality must also be measured in terms of the following:

- Quality of relationships – Are we in bed with the right partners, and are those relationships such that they deliver value for all parties?

- Quality of communication – Is communication transparent and timely? Do our users share sudden changes in plans and business requirements, and do we manage communications with vendors fairly?

- Quality of process – Are our procedures set up to deliver the best outcomes, or do we confuse our users with multiple hoops and surprises?

- Quality of management – Are we investing in our people such that they feel competent and capable to handle the value and volume of spend we commit to them? Are we also dealing with suppliers who have the required maturity at senior levels to make the right decisions that meet our needs?

- Quality of (company) image – Have we dealt with our suppliers and communities such that we are a trusted player? Do we attract the kind of collaborations that drive value?

You will often find that using this approach, it is possible to deliver the same quality at a lower cost, higher quality at the same cost, or higher quality at a lower cost.

QUANTITY

If it were possible to store as much of an item as one would ever need, this would be the way to go! I absolutely hate to walk into a store and be informed that an item I need is out of stock, especially when it's something I have gotten used to and grown to love. This is the challenge from a customer perspective. Now, imagine how much more complex it is for companies to properly manage multiple items of inventory. Any item maintained or held by a business to enable it to meet demand is defined as inventory. The major types are:

- Raw Materials (items used in a manufacturing process e.g., sugar for soft drinks)

- Packing and Packaging Materials (used for packing and storage – bubble wraps, pallets, boxes)

- Work in Progress (WIP) (unfinished items in a production process that need to be further used in manufacturing e.g., parts of a product that need to be assembled)

- Finished Goods (completed items that are ready for sale)

- Maintenance, Repair, and Operations (MRO) (items used up in the production process e.g., bearings, bolts, nuts, and consumables such as tools lubricating oil, and stationery)

- Trading Inventory – Used by the retail industry as they refer to items held for sales to customers.

- Inventory for companies providing services – All kinds of inventory items are required here with varying degrees of usage.

An understanding of inventory and its management is critical to the procurement function because we are tasked to source these items in the right quantity. Too much inventory is a waste as it could lead to restricted cashflows, high storage costs, spoilage, and obsolescence: too little means we risk an out-of-stock situation leading to production downtime, sales/revenue loss, and irrecoverable reputational damage. If we have some accountability for buying items, we must therefore have visibility into the inventory management data and processes.

Inventory management policies are determined by several factors; here in Nigeria, where over 50% of inventory is usually imported, we have the additional challenge of dealing with unpredictable delivery lead times, customs clearing delays, and inland road transportation nightmares. Access to real-time inventory data and sharing the same collaboratively with strategic suppliers is the only way to meet this objective efficiently. If your suppliers don't know what your inventory position and plans are, how would they, in turn, reserve the capacity to meet your demand? Your company is not the only customer they have!

Whether your company has a separate inventory planning/management team or not, procurement should see the data, understand the process, participate in the decisions, and give insights to the supplier side of the equation. In an integrated supply chain, this is the norm; I merely propose these ideas to help with the peculiar situation we are in. Encourage your business leaders to use inventory management software (there are a good number of cost-effective solutions available), ensure the data is updated regularly, and refer to the reports before embarking on sourcing activities. If the user departments put you under pressure to purchase items, request for inventory data and usage as a pre-requisite for attending to purchase requests. Document these as part of your policy, and you will find that there will be some degree of sanity.

You do not want to be the weak link through which your company is losing money, do you?

RIGHT PLACE, RIGHT TIME

The right place refers to the optimal location where the procured items should be delivered by the supplier to be received by the buyer. With a central warehouse to distribute materials or products from, this is not always a huge problem. When your company runs a regional or global operation with multiple manufacturing and distribution locations, you will find that this is crucial in keeping your costs competitive. Where should materials be delivered and produced to achieve nearness to market while keeping costs down? A setup such as this requires long-term collaboration with suppliers to drive value. In some companies, suppliers situate some elements of their production facility within the buyer's factory to be close to other activities involved in the supply network. Certain infrastructure costs are also shared, which, in turn, creates benefits for both parties.

In discussing the right place, it's sometimes worth noting that suppliers with global operations also need to decide on optimum production locations for the buyers' orders, even when these locations are temporary or holding points. They also need to optimise their costs and share some of this value with the client. They are in competition with their peers and may lose business if they don't run a tight ship.

The right time is dependent on proper inventory management because of the element of demand forecasting and planning, but there are other steps which must be considered.

Data, Data, Data – When you analyse the full production and sales cycle, at what point should an order be placed? How much visibility do you have of the end-to-end process such that you can know with certainty that you are delivering value?

Procurement Processing – How long does the procurement process take? Sourcing, negotiations, supplier evaluation, contracting agreements, and approvals.

Supplier Processing and Delivery Lead Times – We often ignore the suppliers' processing times. These should be on the critical path of our project GANTT chart because they also must reserve some production capacity to fulfil your orders.

The right time is also a function of a lean or agile approach to supply chain management.

A lean supply chain is characterised by predictable or steady demand, low variety, long lead times, and relatively high volumes. Production can be scheduled, and forecasts are more accurate than not. An agile supply chain, however, is needed when there are short lead times, a demand for lots of variety, and unpredictable or volatile demand. Agility is all about flexibility, response time, small production runs, minimum order quantities, and the ability to change direction as the trends move.

Martin Christopher, often referred to as the father of supply chain management, has proposed that 'The option for supply chains that cannot reduce lead times is to seek to create a hybrid lean/agile solution'. This means that different aspects of the supply chain need to be managed separately. This is a solution companies in Nigeria might need to explore to stay ahead of the importation challenges.

The imperative of the right place and right time cannot be compromised in the delivery of business objectives. The procurement function is tasked with this responsibility and must partner effectively with relevant internal and external stakeholders to achieve this. Ignoring any one of these elements could have major impacts on the right price and erode value for the organisation. Therefore, procurement must be involved in all areas of the supply chain and the business at large.

RIGHT SOURCE

There were a lot of supplier/source failures at the start of the pandemic, and I observed a lot of panic within supply chains because of the consequences of sourcing predominantly from China and other parts of Asia that were on lockdown. There were disruptions to manufacturing and, in some instances, temporary halts to the flow of goods. While the pandemic is seen as a rare (once-in-a-lifetime) event, the challenges it created for global supply chains are not necessarily new; instead, it only highlighted existing vulnerabilities.

Since the pandemic, selecting a source/supplier has never been more critical. Focusing on immediate value/benefits vs. resilience over the long term may limit a business's growth and ultimately diminish its chances of survival. The pressure of budgets, the attraction of low-cost options, and shortened lead times have driven many buying decisions. However, there are time-tested tools for supplier/source selection which a skilled procurement resource will do well to consider.

Comprehensive sourcing strategies developed for items that make up 80% of supplier spend and critical bottleneck categories are essential to achieving this. This document will contain the following, among others:

- Business Need/Objectives – What is the need driving the sourcing activity? What outcomes are expected from the process?

- Spend Analysis/Trend – Historical spend with suppliers over the last three years ranked in descending order.

- Economic Analysis – All the macro-economic data that impact on the category you are sourcing for.

- Industry Analysis/Porter's Five Forces – A very analytical tool that shows the level of competitiveness in the industry and what levers buyers can pull to shift the balance of power in our favour.

- SWOT Analysis – A 360° perspective of our company and all the possible factors working for and against us.

- Supplier Analysis – Information on all key suppliers for that item, whether we currently buy from them or not and their willingness to do business with us.

- Supplier Portfolio Analysis – How our vendors are classified from a procurement perspective and how we intend to treat them: strategic, bottleneck, leverage, or non-critical. This then feeds into our sourcing choice model.

- Sourcing Plan – How we intend to approach the market; RFQ, RFP, negotiations, etc., and the duration of our agreements.

- Risk Matrix/Mitigation – All known risks that might occur in order of probability and value impact, and the agreed plan to prevent and/or address it.

- Evaluation Criteria – Will be included as part of our bidding documents, providing a clear 'marking scheme' for how we will select our suppliers.

The strategic sourcing document contains other sections and should be valid for three to five years, with stakeholder alignment obtained at different stages of development and signed off by key business leaders. If time and effort is put into having this document for all major categories of spend, your choice of supplier or source will be well-informed. Even with unforeseen incidents like COVID, our degree of confidence in their ability to thrive and continue to meet our needs will be quite high. We will also trust them as they trust us to be a reliable long-term partner.

The right source/supplier is one of the key deliverables of the procurement professional. In the next chapter, I will proceed to discuss the sourcing strategy in detail.

Crafting a Sourcing Strategy

When I joined procurement from an IT project manager role, I received some of the best training available globally. I was working for Procter & Gamble, and they had a very advanced supply chain organisation at the time. The procurement function in the Middle East and Africa was also a close-knit community, meeting regularly, sharing ideas, and attending courses together. The Nigerian manufacturing business was to be modelled after a sister plant in Cairo, Egypt, and this meant we had a 'big brother' organisation to look up to. My first year in procurement was like doing a university degree crash program, plus building a team of smart people who made my work easy. I am forever grateful to the managers I worked with, my team, and the stakeholders who supported me.

Since that time, I have worked for several large and small organisations, led the recruitment of hundreds of people, mentored colleagues and young people, and did business with several companies as a consultant. As procurement evolves into a full-fledged profession, I am inclined to make the comparison with other areas of specialisation.

A medical professional takes time to examine a sick person, asks certain questions, takes their vitals, recommends further tests, and reaches a clear diagnosis of the ailment. Then they prescribe the proper procedures or medication to restore the patient's health.

A lawyer listens to a client, asks pertinent questions, does in-depth research on past cases, builds an argument, and puts up a strong defence in court to secure the client's acquittal or a reduction in punishment, even when they are sometimes guilty of the offence.

An automotive mechanic will listen to the vehicle owner's complaints, run diagnostic tests, take a test drive, listen to the engine, try out different simulations, and isolate the exact fault with the machinery before proposing fixes that will resolve the issue.

An academic will review past papers cited by peers and experts, define a hypothesis, analyse samples, and propose a theory that he/she expects will be tested rigorously by colleagues before the proposal is accepted as an authority in the field.

I can go on.

If procurement is to be established in the field of professions, we must have a unique approach to problem-solving or a methodology that can be tested to arrive at similar solutions regardless of who is running the process.

Some years ago, my team and I conducted a tender that led to a major change in a critical category. The incumbent was going to lose significant business, and they had a stake in multiple companies in the group. As you can imagine, this created some waves within the leadership as they agonised over the decision. As the final proposal went through different levels of approval, we had to make a presentation to the board. The sensitivity of the outcome required that every member of the board sign off, and this prompted a senior board member to request a second opinion of the process. The team based at the Procurement Centre of Excellence would have to do a re-run of the tender process to determine that we did everything by the book.

This may have caused some concern among my colleagues, but not for me. We shared all the documents, and they spent a couple of weeks doing the process.

When they were done, the outcome was the same, they reached the same decision we reached, and the recommendation was approved.

In our evolution as a profession, it is important that we adopt methods like the scientific model where the outcomes we reach can be replicated by anyone. Such outcomes must be based on data and analysis using broadly accepted tools. We may never truly gain the respect we deserve for the work we do until we can demonstrate that our recommendations are a result of a thorough and comprehensive evaluation of different scenarios and possible outcomes.

Even when business exigencies require that a decision be bypassed or delayed, the process needs to be documented to show why the principle-based outcome was put aside in favour of another mandated by the company leadership.

Like we were told in our introduction to complex mathematics, we need to 'show working' or show our work. It is not enough to arrive at the answer, now show us how you got there.

In the last 10 years, there has been a move away from the use of sourcing strategies to the use of sourcing plans in making buying decisions. It is true that the dynamic nature of global markets and the accelerated pace of innovations in technology may have pushed us to make decisions quickly to take advantage of rapid changes.

During the COVID pandemic, scientists were pushed to fast-track the production of a vaccine much quicker than standard testing periods required. This is an example of when exigencies cause professionals to do something out of the ordinary to stem the tide of a crisis or meet a global need. The lesson we learned from this is that the vaccines worked. Yes, it took two to three doses to attain the level of potency required, but the virus is on a decline. If scientific principles had been compromised or shortcuts taken, the credibility of the industry would have been dented irreparably.

In the same way, the fact that we are 'under pressure' does not mean that we abandon the rules and principles that our profession is founded on. We have no excuses for rushed or uninformed decisions, haphazard processes and outcomes that violate compliance guidelines and that can be faulted by an audit.

Like a project management plan, a sourcing plan shows a timeline of tasks to be carried out, a sourcing strategy details the underlying data and models that helped form the conclusions we reached. As we go through the different sections of a sourcing strategy, you will see how it uses models, data, scenario analysis, logic, and sound business judgement to make a case for certain recommendations. It is the one formula that will always give you the same outcome every time you use it.

Sourcing Strategy Elements

Business Need, Capabilities, And Objectives

This section of the sourcing strategy sets the context for the exercise. It is where you break down the 'why' of the effort and use as much data as is available to justify the work done in this area. Describe the category in detail and what the product or service is used for and how it is used in your business, including variants and by-products. State volumes over the past three years and future usage trends (the need driving the sourcing activity). Define the outcomes expected from the process and how these align to the overall strategic direction of your organisation. Specify your business capabilities in terms of capacity for raw material processing, storage, and other requirements that impact on managing the item being sourced. Also mention how the category being sourced feeds into your overall business production and service delivery. Your short-term and long-term goals are the ultimate drivers for the sourcing strategy.

Linking Procurement to Business Needs Involves:

Identifying the organisation's business needs by assessing the organisation's current and future requirements for goods and services, as well as identifying any potential risks or vulnerabilities in the supply chain.

I often listen to colleagues express concern about the lack of information from the business units, which puts procurement on the back foot as far as requisitions are concerned. This is one of the phases a procurement Function will have to pass through on the journey to maturity. I propose the following steps to address this gap:

Periodic meetings between department heads – The head of procurement should initiate periodic meetings with all department heads in the spend areas under coverage. The meetings should discuss the general health of the stakeholder relationship, pending issues that need to be resolved, upcoming priorities for the department, big-ticket items being planned, ways of working, and other business.

Category managers should attend departmental strategic meetings – These meetings will usually give key insights into the plans of the user department, which will help procurement prepare to handle related requisitions when they eventually appear in our inboxes. An understanding of user department's long-term plans will feed directly into procurement sourcing strategies.

Review monthly/quarterly requirements are in line with annual goals – In addition to aligning strategies, it is important to stay on track as business requirements change. Agreements with suppliers and contractual obligations are directly affected by these changes and periodic reviews are one way to manage expectations effectively. It is always better to overcommunicate.

Update on key market changes for affected categories – The level of information sharing between procurement and user departments extends to market updates. Both parties should be keen to exchange relevant information that affects their category, especially as it relates to innovation in the market, changes in the competitive landscape, new entrants to the market, and regulatory and environmental changes, etc.

Joint negotiations for technical categories – Now this is one activity that a lot of colleagues seem surprised to hear. I am an advocate for team negotiations in complex/technical transactions. I've found that it is one way for me to deepen my knowledge in the category and become an 'expert'. This is the 'age of collaboration', and we cannot achieve anything significant on our own. It is immature to think that a commercial negotiation will effectively drive down prices without reference to the technical elements that build up the total cost. A deep understanding of the category will enhance the negotiations and give every party a transparent perspective of the issues at stake.

Joint team bonding and reward sessions – When a procurement category manager has been successful in delivering a project, it is only fair that such an individual is celebrated in departmental team reward sessions. I also request for key stakeholders to be invited to procurement team bonding sessions. We are working together, and every opportunity to spend time together should be sought after and cherished.

Spend Analysis

I already mentioned that you do sourcing strategies for the categories that account for 80% of spend. The rigour and time involved are such that you cannot do it for everything. It is a visual representation of your suppliers and categories (analysed from highest to lowest spend) over the last three years. There are several spend analysis tools that can access your database to extract this data, or you can use a simple excel worksheet after you have received details of all purchase order spend accounts payable, data from your procurement software, the general ledger from finance, and your enterprise resource planning database.

Be clear with why you need the data – There are other purposes to analysing spend apart from developing a sourcing strategy e.g., specific cost reduction projects, detecting and eliminating maverick spend, using it as a basis for forecasts, and as part of a risk management/mitigation exercise.

Clean/organise the data – The data will then need to be consolidated into a format that makes it easy to manipulate. You will understand this especially if you're using excel as the formulas will only work when the data is in a relatable format. Check for errors, fix duplicates and other inconsistencies, then arrange them in whatever order makes sense.

Group categories and consolidate supplier spend – Many organisations have certain suppliers dealing in multiple spend areas, so you will want to determine that the data is captured accurately. Total suppliers' spend per category, total spend per category, and the top twenty percent for each analysis will give you a clear picture of areas you want to dig deeper into. There are many standards to help you categorise spend but use the one that works for your area of business.

Now do the spend analysis – Sometimes, just seeing the data presented in this manner reveals so much about your business that it leads you to make immediate decisions about how you proceed with certain categories. The first time I did this exercise, some vendors appeared in my top twenty percent who were not considered strategic; but because we had not been tracking spend, and they operated in more than one category, we were spending huge sums of money on them. In some cases, the decision will be to start treating them as strategic.

You will also identify the 80% of vendors accountable for 20% of spend. This decision on categorisation will have to be made with the use of other tools as well, and we will discuss these as we progress. Always bear in mind that the purpose of the spend analysis (what you want to use it for) will determine how you do the data manipulation and what it reports to you. For instance, if you are doing a spend analysis to help you with a Kraljic model or a supplier portfolio analysis so you can classify your categories/vendors and treat them appropriately, you will want to present the data in such a way that it shows spend vs. the number of purchase orders issued per period layered over the supply risk. This way, you will be able to put each category in its proper classification.

For the sourcing strategy, however, you will be doing the spend analysis to also justify the approach you will take towards that category. This brings me to a key point:

You do not only do sourcing strategies for items in the strategic quadrant of the Kraljic matrix.

A sourcing strategy can be developed for items in the routine/leverage category, where you define your approach using the data you gather from the industry. It is a strategy because it guides your buying approach in that category for the next three to five years. For instance, if stationeries are classified as routine in your Krailjc model, but the spend is significant because of the size of your business, you can develop a sourcing strategy that outlines how you intend to source those items even if the approach is to use catalogues, eProcurement cards, bulk purchase orders, eAuctions, etc.

Sourcing strategies take a medium to long-term view using all the information available at the time. You can always revise them as market changes occur. As such, if business needs require significant change in a particular category, you may need to re-do the spend analysis and repeat the process outlined above to gain new insights.

Economic Analysis

Economic analysis is a method of evaluating the costs and benefits of a particular course of action or decision. It is commonly used to assess the feasibility or desirability of a project, policy, or investment. It involves collecting and analysing data on various economic factors, such as prices, production levels, employment, and GDP, in order to understand how they influence economic activity so you can make informed decisions about economic policy or business strategy and estimating the costs of a particular action or decision and comparing them to the expected benefits or returns. Economic analysis can be used to inform a wide range of decisions, including investment decisions, policy decisions, and business decisions. It is a key tool for understanding the potential impacts and consequences of different courses of action.

There are several different approaches to economic analysis, including microeconomics and macroeconomics. Microeconomics focuses on the behaviour of individual firms and households, while macroeconomics looks at the whole economy.

There are several types of economic analysis that may be used in a sourcing strategy, depending on the specific decision or situation being evaluated. Some common types of economic analysis include:

Cost-benefit analysis: Used to evaluate the potential costs and benefits of a policy, project, or decision. It involves comparing the costs of a particular action or decision with the benefits that are expected to result from it. The goal is to determine whether the benefits outweigh the costs and to what extent. To conduct a cost-benefit analysis, it is necessary to identify all the costs and benefits associated with a particular action or decision. This includes both tangible costs and benefits, such as the financial costs of implementing a policy or the monetary value of the benefits that will result from it, as well as intangible costs and benefits, such as the social and environmental impacts of the policy. Once all the costs and benefits have been identified and quantified, they can be compared to determine the overall net benefit of the action or decision. If the benefits are greater than the costs, the action or decision may be worthwhile. If the costs are greater than the benefits, the action or decision may not be a good use of resources.

Cost-effectiveness analysis: The method used to evaluate the relative efficiency of two or more alternatives or options. It involves comparing the costs of each option with the benefits or outcomes that are expected to determine which option represents the best value. Unlike cost-benefit analysis, which measures the net benefits of an action or decision by comparing the total costs to the total benefits, cost-effectiveness analysis compares the costs of different options to the benefits or outcomes that they produce. The goal is to identify the option that produces the most benefits or outcomes for the least cost.

To conduct a cost-effectiveness analysis, it is necessary to identify all the costs associated with each option, as well as the benefits or outcomes that are expected to result from each option. These costs and benefits can be expressed in different units of measure, such as dollars, lives saved, or quality-adjusted life years (QALYs).

Cost-effectiveness analysis is often used in policymaking, healthcare decision-making, and other contexts to help determine the most efficient and effective course of action. It can be useful when there are limited resources available, and it is necessary to make trade-offs between different options.

Break-even analysis: This is a method used to determine the point at which the costs of a project or business venture are equal to the revenues generated by it. The goal of break-even analysis is to identify the level of production or sales at which a business will be able to cover all its costs and begin to generate a profit. To conduct a break-even analysis, it is necessary to identify the total fixed costs associated with a project or business venture, as well as the variable costs per unit of production or sales. The fixed costs are costs that do not change regardless of the level of production or sales, such as rent, insurance, and salaries. The variable costs are costs that vary with the level of production or sales, such as raw materials and labour. Once the fixed and variable costs have been identified, it is possible to calculate the break-even point by dividing the total fixed costs by the difference between the price per unit and the variable cost per unit. This will give the number of units that must be produced or sold to break even. Break-even analysis is often used to help businesses determine the minimum level of production or sales that they need to achieve to become profitable, as well as to assess the financial feasibility of a project or business venture. It can also be used to determine the optimal pricing strategy for a product or service.

Market analysis: This is the process of gathering and analysing information about the market for goods or services that an organisation needs to acquire. The goal of procurement market analysis is to identify potential suppliers, understand their capabilities and capacities, and determine the best options for procuring the goods or services that the organisation needs. There are several key elements that organisations typically consider when conducting market analysis:

- Market size: The size of the market for the goods or services being procured, including the number of potential suppliers and the overall demand for the products.

- Market dynamics: The forces that shape the market, such as competition, supply and demand, and economic conditions.

- Market trends: The direction in which the market is moving, including changes in demand, prices, and the competitive landscape.

- Supplier capabilities: The capabilities and capacities of potential suppliers, including their ability to meet the organisation's needs in terms of quantity, quality, delivery times, and any other relevant factors.

- Market risks: The potential risks and uncertainties associated with procuring goods or services from a particular market, including financial risks, legal risks, and regulatory risks.

- Make vs. buy analysis: A process that helps organisations decide whether to produce a product or service in-house (make) or to purchase it from an external supplier (buy). This analysis is often used when an organisation is considering whether to outsource a particular function or when it is deciding whether to produce a product or component internally. In conducting a make vs. buy analysis, an organisation will consider several factors, including cost, quality, capacity, expertise, and risk. For example, if an organisation is considering whether to outsource the production of a component, it might consider the cost of producing the component in-house versus the cost of purchasing it from a supplier. It might also consider the quality of the component produced in-house versus the quality of the component purchased from a supplier.

Other tools and techniques that can be used include statistical analysis, mathematical modelling, and computer simulations. Economic analysis is often used to inform policy decisions, business strategy, and financial planning.

In the sourcing strategy, an economic analysis provides context for your recommendations because every decision impacts the bottom line. When you go seeking approvals for your strategy, the outcome must make economic sense in the short or long term. We are a commercial function, and this must reflect in the way we go about getting results. Certain decisions may hurt the company's profitability over time, and only a well-laid-out economic analysis will show this. You should request help from your finance team when doing this because they are privy to commercial data that you might not have.

Lastly, always present your recommendations as options, with short/long-term profit and cost implications for each one. Business leaders like to know that they made decisions based on ALL the information available at the time. Our duty is to present the data, show them how we get there, highlight our preferred scenario, and leave them to debate healthily until they arrive at a decision.

Industry Analysis

Industry analysis is the process of evaluating the opportunities, threats, and competitive landscape of a specific industry. It involves examining various aspects of an industry, including the market size and growth rate, the types of products and services offered, the competitive dynamics, and the regulatory environment.

Conducting an industry analysis can help a business understand the trends and forces that are shaping its market, identify the key players and their strengths and weaknesses, and develop strategies to compete effectively. It can also help a business assess the potential risks and opportunities associated with entering or expanding in a particular industry.

There are several tools and techniques that can be used to conduct an industry analysis, including:

PESTLIED: This framework is used to analyse the external factors that can impact an industry. PESTLIED stands for political, economic, sociocultural, technological, legal, international, environmental, and demographic. These factors can be used to assess the opportunities and threats that a company or industry may face in executing a strategy.

Political factors refer to the government's policies, regulations, and legal frameworks that can impact an industry. These can include things like tax policies, trade regulations, and labour laws.

Economic factors include the state of the economy, including economic growth, exchange rates, and inflation. These can impact an industry through factors such as consumer spending, the cost of raw materials, and the availability of credit.

Sociocultural factors include cultural values and demographics, which can affect consumer behaviour. These can include things like cultural norms, population growth, and changes in the age structure of the population.

Technological factors include the impact of new technologies on an industry, such as the adoption of new software or machinery. These can drive innovation and increase efficiency but can also disrupt existing business models.

Legal factors include laws and regulations that can impact an industry, such as environmental regulations or consumer protection laws. These can create opportunities or challenges for businesses operating in the industry.

International factors include the impact of global trade and international relations on an industry. These can include things like changes in trade policies, currency exchange rates, and the actions of foreign governments.

Environmental factors include the physical and natural environment in which an industry operates, such as climate and natural resources.

These can impact the cost and availability of raw materials, as well as the environmental impact of the industry.

Demographic factors include the characteristics of the population, such as age, gender, and education level. These can impact consumer demand for certain products and services.

Another useful industry analysis tool that is more relevant to the development of sourcing strategies by procurement is the:

Porter's Five Forces: This framework, developed by management theorist Michael Porter, identifies five forces that shape the competitive landscape of an industry: the bargaining power of suppliers, the bargaining power of buyers, the threat of new entrants, the threat of substitutes, and the intensity of competitive rivalry.

Bargaining Power of Suppliers

The bargaining power of suppliers refers to the influence that suppliers have over the price and availability of the raw materials, components, or services that a business needs to produce its products or deliver its services. In general, the greater the bargaining power of suppliers, the more influence they have over the prices that a business must pay for the inputs it needs.

There are several factors that can affect the bargaining power of suppliers, including:

The number of suppliers: If there are many suppliers offering similar products or services, it can be difficult for any one supplier to wield significant power over prices. Conversely, if there are few suppliers or only one dominant supplier, they may be able to exert more influence over prices.

The uniqueness of the products or services: If a business relies on a unique product or service that is not available from any other supplier, the supplier may have more bargaining power.

The relative size of the supplier: A larger supplier may have more bargaining power than a smaller one, especially if it is a key supplier to the business.

The cost of switching to a new supplier: If it would be expensive or time-consuming for a business to switch to a new supplier, the current supplier may have more bargaining power.

The degree of differentiation: If a supplier's products or services are highly differentiated or have strong brand recognition, they may be able to command higher prices and have more bargaining power.

Understanding the bargaining power of suppliers is important for businesses because it can affect the prices they must pay for inputs and, in turn, their profitability.

Here are some questions that a business might ask to determine the bargaining power of its suppliers:

- How many suppliers are there for the products or services that the business needs?
- Are the products or services offered by the suppliers unique, or are they widely available from other sources?
- How large are the suppliers compared to the business?
- How easily could the business switch to a different supplier if needed?
- What are the costs and risks associated with switching to a new supplier?
- How differentiated are the products or services offered by the suppliers?
- Do the suppliers have strong brand recognition or customer loyalty?
- What is the level of competition among the suppliers?

- How dependent is the business on the products or services provided by the suppliers?

- What is the overall state of the industry in which the suppliers operate, and how does this affect their bargaining power?

Answering these questions can help you understand the factors that are influencing the bargaining power of its suppliers and assess the potential risks and opportunities associated with its sourcing decisions.

Bargaining Power of Buyers

The bargaining power of buyers refers to the influence that customers have over the prices and terms of the products or services that they purchase. In general, the greater the bargaining power of buyers, the more influence they have over the prices that a business can charge for its products or services.

There are several factors that can affect the bargaining power of buyers, including:

The number of buyers: If there are many buyers in the market, it can be difficult for any one buyer to wield significant power over prices. Conversely, if there are few buyers or only one dominant buyer, they may be able to exert more influence over prices.

The size of the buyers: Larger buyers may have more bargaining power than smaller ones, especially if they are significant customers for the business.

The importance of the products or services to the buyers: If the products or services offered by the business are critical to the buyers' operations, they may have more bargaining power.

The degree of differentiation: If the products or services offered by the business are highly differentiated or have strong brand recognition, the business may be able to command higher prices and have more bargaining power.

The availability of substitutes: If there are many substitute products or services available, buyers may have more bargaining power.

Questions that a buyer might ask to determine the bargaining power of its buyers include the following:

- How many buyers are there for the products or services that the business offers?

- How large are the buyers compared to the business?

- How important are the products or services offered by the business to the buyers?

- How differentiated are the products or services offered by the business?

- Do the products or services offered by the business have strong brand recognition or customer loyalty?

- Are there many substitute products or services available to the buyers?

- What is the level of competition among the buyers?

- How dependent are the buyers on the products or services offered by the business?

- What is the overall state of the industry in which the buyers operate, and how does this affect their bargaining power?

Answering these questions helps a procurement professional to understand the factors that are influencing the bargaining power of buyers within the industry and assess the potential risks and opportunities associated with its pricing and sales strategies.

The Threat of New Entrants

The threat of new entrants refers to the potential for new businesses to enter a market and compete with existing players. In general, the greater the threat of new entrants, the more difficult it is for existing businesses to maintain their market share and profitability.

Factors that can affect the threat of new entrants include:

Barriers to entry: These are the obstacles or costs that a new business must overcome to enter a market. Some examples of barriers to entry include economies of scale, capital requirements, regulatory barriers, access to distribution channels, and customer loyalty to existing brands.

The intensity of competitive rivalry: If the existing players in a market are engaged in intense competition, it can be more difficult for a new entrant to gain a foothold.

The power of suppliers and buyers: If the suppliers or buyers in an industry have a strong bargaining position, they may be able to limit the ability of new entrants to succeed.

The overall attractiveness of the industry: If an industry is experiencing strong growth or is highly profitable, it may be more attractive to new entrants.

Understanding the threat of new entrants is important for businesses because it can affect their ability to compete and maintain their market share.

You can ask and answer the following questions to help to determine the threat of new entrants/players in the industry:

- What are the barriers to entry in the market?
- How intense is the competition among existing players in the market?
- What is the bargaining power of suppliers and buyers in the market?
- Is the market growing or declining, and what are the trends in the industry?

- What is the overall attractiveness of the industry for new entrants?

- Are there any regulatory or legal barriers that would prevent new entrants from entering the market?

- What is the level of customer loyalty to existing brands in the market?

- How easy is it for new entrants to access distribution channels and other necessary resources?

- How much capital would be required for a new entrant to enter the market and be competitive?

- Are there any incumbent firms with significant competitive advantages that would make it difficult for a new entrant to succeed?

The Threat of Substitutes

The threat of substitutes refers to the potential for consumers to switch to alternative products or services that can fulfil the same need. In general, the greater the threat of substitutes, the more pressure there is on businesses to lower their prices or improve the value of their offerings to stay competitive.

There are several factors that can affect the threat of substitutes, including:

The availability of substitutes: If there are many substitute products or services available, it can be more difficult for businesses to maintain their market share and pricing power.

The price and performance of substitutes: If the substitute products or services are cheaper or offer better value, it can be more difficult for businesses to maintain their market share and pricing power.

The switching costs: If it is expensive or inconvenient for consumers to switch to a substitute product or service, it can reduce the threat of substitutes.

The degree of differentiation: If the products or services offered by a business are highly differentiated or have strong brand recognition, it may be able to command higher prices and have more pricing power, despite the presence of substitutes.

Understanding the threat of substitutes is important for businesses because it can affect their ability to maintain their market share and pricing power.

Questions you can ask to determine the threat of substitutes in its market:

- How many substitute products or services are available in the market?
- How do the prices and performance of the substitute products or services compare to those offered by the business?
- What are the switching costs for consumers to switch to substitute products or services?
- How differentiated are the products or services offered by the business?
- Do the products or services offered by the business have strong brand recognition or customer loyalty?
- How easy is it for consumers to access and use substitute products or services?
- How likely are consumers to switch to substitute products or services if the price or value of the business's offerings changes?
- What is the overall state of the industry in which the substitutes operate, and how does this affect their threat to the business?

The Intensity of Competitive Rivalry

The intensity of competitive rivalry refers to the level of competition among the businesses in an industry. In general, the higher the intensity of competitive rivalry, the more difficult it is for businesses to maintain their market share and profitability.

Factors that can affect the intensity of competitive rivalry:

The number of competitors: If there are many competitors in a market, it can lead to more intense competition as each business tries to win customers and market share.

The similarity of the products or services offered: If the products or services offered by different businesses are similar, it can lead to more intense competition as consumers have more choices and businesses must differentiate themselves in order to stand out.

The level of excess capacity: If there is excess capacity in a market, it can lead to more intense competition as businesses try to find ways to sell their excess production.

The level of differentiation: If the products or services offered by different businesses are highly differentiated, it may reduce the intensity of competition as consumers are less likely to switch to a substitute product or service.

The exit barriers: If it is difficult or costly for businesses to exit a market, it can lead to more intense competition as businesses try to recover their investments and make a profit.

The answers to the following questions can help to determine the intensity of competitive rivalry in the industry under consideration:

- How many competitors are there in the market?
- How similar are the products or services offered by the competitors?
- How much excess capacity is there in the market?

- How differentiated are the products or services offered by the competitors?
- What are the exit barriers for businesses in the market?
- How intense is the competition among the competitors in terms of pricing, marketing, and other strategies?
- How does the competitive landscape in the market compare to other industries or markets?
- Are there any dominant competitors with significant market share or competitive advantages?
- How does the competitive environment in the market affect the profitability of the businesses operating in it?

The outcome of the Porter's model will guide the approach to implementing a sourcing strategy.

SWOT Analysis

A SWOT analysis is a tool used to evaluate the strengths, weaknesses, opportunities, and threats (SWOT) of a business or project. It is a strategic planning tool that helps businesses assess their internal and external environments and identify factors that can impact their success.

To conduct a SWOT analysis, a business or organisation typically follows these steps:

Identify the business's strengths: These are the internal factors that give the business an advantage over its competitors. Examples of strengths might include strong brand recognition, a highly skilled workforce, proprietary technology, or a strong financial position.

Identify the business's weaknesses: These are the internal factors that may hinder the business's ability to achieve its goals. Examples of weaknesses might include a lack of financial resources, outdated technology, poor customer service, or a lack of differentiation from competitors.

Identify the business's opportunities: These are the external factors that the business can take advantage of to achieve its goals. Examples of opportunities might include market trends, changes in technology, new regulations, or shifts in consumer behaviour.

Identify the business's threats: These are the external factors that may pose a risk to the business's success. Examples of threats might include competition, changes in customer preferences, economic downturns, or regulatory changes.

By conducting a SWOT analysis, a business or organisation can better understand its internal and external environments and develop strategies to capitalise on its strengths and opportunities while minimising its weaknesses and threats.

Strengths

A business's strengths are the areas where it excels or performs better than its competitors or industry benchmarks. Some common examples of strengths in a business include:

Strong financial performance: This could include high profits, low debt levels, and positive cash flow.

High-quality products or services: This could include innovative offerings, a strong track record of customer satisfaction, or a unique value proposition.

Valuable resources: This could include financial resources, talented employees, valuable partnerships, or access to unique technologies.

Efficient processes: This could include fast turnaround times, low levels of waste, or high levels of productivity.

Strong brand presence or reputation: This could include high levels of customer awareness or loyalty or a positive image within the industry.

Resilient supply chain or operations: This could include diversified sources of supply or production facilities or robust contingency plans in place to mitigate risks.

Ability to adapt to change: This could include a track record of successfully navigating technological advancements or shifts in consumer preferences.

Having strong business strengths can give a company a competitive advantage and set it up for long-term success.

Ask and answer the following questions to determine a business's strengths.

- What products or services does the business offer, and how do they differentiate from competitors?
- What is the business's target market, and how well does it understand and meet the needs of its customers?
- What resources does the business have at its disposal, such as financial resources, talented employees, or valuable partnerships?
- What processes and systems does the business have in place to ensure efficiency and effectiveness?
- What is the business's track record of success, and how has it performed financially over the past few years?
- What challenges has the business faced and overcome in the past, and how has it adapted to change?
- How does the business measure and track its performance, and how does it use data and analytics to inform decision-making?
- What reputation does the business have within its industry and among its customers?

Weaknesses

Poor financial performance: This could include low profits, high debt levels, or negative cash flow.

Weaknesses in products or services: This could include a lack of innovation, low quality, or limited appeal to customers.

Limited resources: This could include a lack of financial resources, skilled employees, or technology.

Inefficient processes: This could include slow turnaround times, high levels of waste, or low levels of productivity.

Weak brand presence or reputation: This could include low levels of customer awareness or loyalty or a negative image within the industry.

Vulnerabilities in supply chain or operations: This could include a reliance on a single supplier or production facility or a lack of redundancy in key processes.

Inability to adapt to change: This could include a slow response to technological advancements or shifts in consumer preferences.

It is important to evaluate our weaknesses because this helps us to identify areas of vulnerability that the competition can take advantage of. We may also want to eliminate activities in these areas and focus on where our strengths lie.

To determine a business's weaknesses, answers to the following questions can provide some insight:

- Who are the business's main competitors, and how do they compare in terms of products or services offered, pricing, market share, and customer satisfaction?
- What challenges is the business currently facing, and how is it addressing them?

- What processes or systems does the business have in place, and are there any areas that could be improved or streamlined?
- What is the business's track record of financial performance, and are there any warning signs of potential financial trouble?
- Does the business have any vulnerabilities in its supply chain or operations that could disrupt its ability to serve customers?
- How is the business adapting to industry changes or technological advancements, and is it keeping up with competitors in this regard?
- Does the business have any weaknesses in its marketing or sales efforts, such as a weak brand presence or low customer acquisition rates?
- How does the business gather and use customer feedback, and is there anything that consistently comes up as an area for improvement?

Threats

A business's threats refer to the external factors that could potentially harm the business or negatively impact its performance. These threats could be external events or developments, such as economic downturns or regulatory changes, or they could be competitive pressures from other businesses.

Some examples of threats that a business might face include:

Economic downturns: Economic downturns can lead to reduced consumer spending, which can impact the business's sales and profitability.

Regulatory changes: Changes in regulations or policies can impact the business's operations and profitability, especially if the business is not well-prepared to adapt to the changes.

Competition: The presence of strong competitors can make it difficult for a business to attract and retain customers, which can impact its sales and profitability.

Changes in consumer preferences: Shifts in consumer preferences, such as a move towards more environmentally friendly products, can impact the demand for the business's products or services.

Changes in technology: Rapid advances in technology can disrupt traditional business models and create new competitors, which can impact the business's competitiveness.

Natural disasters: Natural disasters, such as storms or earthquakes, can disrupt the business's operations and supply chain, which can impact its ability to meet customer demand and maintain profitability.

You must see how any of the above situations can affect sourcing strategy decisions. Our duty is to bring these scenarios and the probability of occurrence to the attention of senior leaders. By doing so, the business can minimise the potential impact of external threats and position itself for long-term success.

To determine a business's threats, you can ask and answer the following questions:

- What are the external factors that could impact the business? This could include economic conditions, regulatory changes, or geopolitical events. How vulnerable is the business to these factors?

- What are the business's competitors doing? Are there new competitors entering the market or established competitors expanding their offerings or market share?

- What are the changes in consumer preferences or needs? Are there shifts in consumer demand that could impact the business's products or services?

- What technological advancements or disruptions could impact the business? Are there new technologies or business models that could disrupt the business's operations or market position?

- What are the potential natural disasters or other external events that could disrupt the business's operations? How prepared is the business to handle these types of disruptions?

- What are the business's strengths and weaknesses? How can the business leverage its strengths to mitigate potential threats, and how can it address its weaknesses to reduce vulnerability?

The answers to these questions can help you identify areas for improvement and develop strategies to address potential threats.

Opportunities

The potential opportunities that are available to help the business grow, expand, and succeed are listed here. These can be internal opportunities, such as identifying and capitalising on new markets or products, or external opportunities, such as partnerships or acquisitions.

Some examples of opportunities that a business might pursue include:

Diversifying the product or service offerings: A business might identify new products or services that it can offer to its customers, which can help it expand its customer base and revenue streams.

Entering new markets: A business might identify new geographical or demographic markets to target, which can help it expand its customer base and increase its sales.

Partnering with other businesses: A business might identify opportunities to form partnerships with other businesses, which can provide access to new resources, expertise, and networks.

Acquiring other businesses: A business might identify opportunities to acquire other businesses, which can provide access to new products, technologies, and customers.

Leveraging technology: A business might identify opportunities to leverage technology, such as by developing new digital products or services or by using technology to streamline internal processes.

Here are some questions that you might ask to determine a business's opportunities:

- What are the current trends in the industry? Are there new products or services that are gaining popularity? Are there new technologies that could be leveraged to improve the business?

- What are the customer needs and preferences? Are there unmet needs or untapped markets that the business could address?

- What are the competitors doing? Is the business keeping pace with its competitors, or is there room to differentiate?

- What are the business's strengths and weaknesses? How can the business leverage its strengths to take advantage of opportunities, and how can it address its weaknesses to mitigate potential threats?

- What are the external factors that could impact the business? This could include economic conditions, regulatory changes, or geopolitical events. How can the business adapt to these changes or take advantage of them?

- What resources does the business have available to pursue new opportunities? This could include financial resources, personnel, technology, or physical assets.

- How do the business's mission and vision align with potential opportunities? Is the business willing and able to pivot or adapt its direction to pursue new opportunities?

By asking these questions, you can gain a better understanding of the opportunities that are available to the business and how the business can capitalise on them.

Please note that all the above discussions have to be developed in context of the category you are developing the sourcing strategy for; otherwise, it will be useless. So please ensure that the information you gather is relevant to the category items and industry you are addressing.

Market Research

This involves gathering and analysing data on market trends, consumer behaviour, and industry performance.

Market research is the process of gathering and analysing information about a market, including its size, demographics, preferences, and trends. Market research is typically conducted in order to inform marketing and business strategies and to identify opportunities for growth and expansion.

There are several methods that businesses can use to conduct market research, including:

Surveys: Surveys can be conducted online, by phone, or in person, and they typically involve asking a sample of consumers questions about their preferences, habits, and attitudes towards products or services.

Focus groups: Focus groups involve bringing a small group of consumers together to discuss and provide feedback on a product or service. This can provide valuable insights into consumer attitudes and preferences.

Online analytics: Businesses can use online analytics tools, such as Google Analytics, to track website traffic and user behaviour, which can provide valuable insights into consumer behaviour.

Interviews: Businesses can conduct in-depth interviews with consumers or industry experts to gather more detailed information about a market.

Observational research: Observational research involves observing consumers in their natural environment, such as in a store or online, to understand their behaviour and preferences.

Competitive Analysis

This involves examining the strategies and tactics of competitors, including their products and services, pricing, marketing, and distribution channels. Someone might ask why this is important, and correctly so because it is the primary role of marketing and sales to conduct competitive analysis; however, the consensus is that the competition is among supply chains. Every decision made by members of our profession has a direct impact on the bottom line, which in turn has an impact on the price, quality, and speed to market (overall competitiveness) of the company's products and services.

Competitive analysis is the process of evaluating the strengths and weaknesses of your competitors' supply chains to understand their position in the industry and identify opportunities for differentiation. It involves comparing your business's supply chain to others in your industry or market, looking at factors such as their products or services, pricing, technology, processes, and supply base.

There are several ways to conduct a competitive analysis, including:

Analysing the competition's website and marketing materials: Look for information about their products or services, pricing, and target audience.

Researching industry reports and trade publications: These sources often provide information about competitors, including market share and financial performance.

Asking suppliers: Gathering feedback from suppliers about your competitors can provide valuable insights into how they perceive the competition. Note that you can only gather information of a general nature through this method, so you do not unwittingly violate existing NDAs in place. Suppliers who freely share confidential information about their clients cannot be relied upon.

Visiting suppliers: Visiting suppliers' facilities and listening to presentations about their business can be very insightful as a source of information.

Monitoring social media and online reviews: Keeping track of what suppliers are saying about your competitors on social media and review sites can help you understand their strengths and weaknesses.

The goal of competitive analysis is to understand the competitive landscape to develop strategies to differentiate your business and position it for success. By understanding your competitors and their strengths and weaknesses, you can make informed decisions about how to best optimise your supply base and grow your business.

Supplier Analysis

Supplier analysis is the process of evaluating and assessing the capabilities, reliability, and performance of a company's suppliers. The goal of supplier analysis is to identify potential risks and opportunities associated with each supplier and to determine the best strategies for managing these relationships.

The supplier analysis helps us to develop a superior understanding of supplier capability and use that understanding to deliver that supplier's goods, services, technologies, etc., to provide optimum total value results to the business.

The Carter's 10 Cs model provides guidelines for gathering information used to conduct supplier analysis:

1. Competency

To evaluate supplier competency, make a thorough assessment of their capabilities, and measure them against your needs. Then listen to what other clients think. How happy are they with the supplier? Have they encountered any problems? And find out why they changed suppliers.

Look for companies whose needs and values are similar to yours to ensure that the information you gather is relevant to your organisation.

2. Capacity

Does the supplier have enough capacity to handle your company's and others' requirements? How quickly will they be able to respond to your needs and supply fluctuations in the market?

Your assessment of capacity should include production equipment, staff, storage, inventory, and the ability of the supplier to respond quickly and effectively to changes in demand or other factors.

3. Commitment

Evidence of supplier's commitment to safety, quality, and other professional standards is found in their involvement in programs such as ISO 9001 or Six Sigma and other cultural or procurement excellence programs.

If you're planning to build a long-term relationship with them, it is important for the supplier to show that they will be committed to you, as a client, throughout the duration of the partnership. Remember that they have commitments to other clients as well, so this obligation should cover everyone.

4. Control

Companies you deal with must show that they are in control of their supply chain, finances, processes, and systems. Evidence of this is that you are dealing with the owners and decision-makers and that they are not wholly or partly controlled by another organisation. Also check for any liens by financial institutions and regulatory agencies.

5. Cash

The supplier's liquidity or cash-positive status is a good indicator of their ability to manage your requirements. They will also be able to survive tough economic downturns and unexpected changes in requirements. Can they handle additional requirements with relative ease, or are they operating at the limits of their financial capacity? Their cash position is a very good measure of their financial health.

6. Cost

Your supplier's costs are your costs, so you want to study these closely and make comparisons across similar organisations. Evaluate the cost of the product or service that this supplier provides; how does it compare with the other options that you're considering?

By itself, the price you pay for a product or service cannot determine your choice of supplier. Cost should always be looked at over the life cycle of the item, and we will be looking at the total ownership cost concept in further detail later in this book.

7. Consistency

Another factor to consider is the reliability of suppliers over the long term. How have they performed with other clients? Can the records demonstrate that they consistently deliver against agreed parameters, or do they hover up and down the scale of parameters they are required to deliver against?

Is their technology tried and tested, or are they experimenting with new ideas? Nothing wrong with this except that the client needs to be aware and plan for how such products/services are released into the market.

8. Culture

Workplace culture is another factor businesses need to consider in their engagement with suppliers. Every organisation has accepted norms within the work environment and the community in general. Understanding and determining that your values align is a key requirement for a relationship. Our culture guides how we make decisions and is a core driver for the performance level of any organisation. It also forms the basis for who and how we relate to others. Business is ultimately about people, and companies will build the strongest relationships with suppliers who share their core values. Suppliers who are recognised for certain cultural values similar to yours will most likely do well as long-term partners.

9. Clean

I like to think that this standard refers to how well organisations treat their workplace facilities first. Having good HSE practices should lead to sustainable investments in the environment and a dedicated effort to reduce carbon footprints and fight climate change. As such, suppliers who are focused on the use of environmentally friendly materials and green energy should earn a right to receive business. Have they earned any credentials in environmental sustainability? Do they have a reputation for their efforts to reduce waste? How do they treat their people? What CSR activities have they been engaged in?

10. Communication

Another critical element in supplier analysis is their communication infrastructure and style. Will you be talking to a decision-maker each time, or do they have a complex decision-making hierarchy? How quickly and how well do they share important information? Will they be using methods and media that work well with your company? How often will you review progress and discuss updates? The lack of constant communication can derail important projects and relationships, so bear this in mind as you review this element.

Portfolio Analysis

The Kraljic matrix is a tool used in supply chain management to analyse the procurement portfolio of an organisation. It was developed by Peter Kraljic in 1983 and is based on the idea that different types of products or materials that an organisation procures will have different levels of impact on the organisation's profitability and risk. It is also used to guide our sourcing approach to these categories because you really cannot drive value if you treat all items and suppliers the same.

The Kraljic matrix divides the procurement portfolio into four categories:

Leverage items: These are items that have a low impact on the organisation's profitability but are purchased in large quantities. They are usually readily available and have low levels of risk.

Leverage items are typically considered to be less critical to the organisation's operations and may be more readily available on the market. As a result, the organisation may have more bargaining power with suppliers of these items, which can be used to negotiate favourable prices or terms.

Managing leverage items effectively can help the organisation to increase its profitability by reducing costs. This may involve standardising on certain products, seeking out lower-cost suppliers, or implementing inventory management strategies to optimise the procurement of these items.

Here are some questions that an organisation might ask to identify leverage items in its procurement portfolio:

- What are the items that the organisation purchases in large quantities?
- What is the impact of these items on the organisation's profitability?
- How readily available are these items on the market?
- What is the level of risk associated with obtaining these items (e.g., are there any potential shortages or price fluctuations)?
- How much bargaining power does the organisation have with suppliers of these items?
- How important are these items to the organisation's operations?
- Can the organisation easily switch to alternative suppliers if necessary?

Bottleneck items: These are items that have a high impact on the organisation's profitability and are purchased in large quantities. They may be more difficult to obtain and have a higher level of risk.

In the context of the Kraljic matrix, bottleneck items are those that have a high rating on the organisation's risk footprint and are purchased in small to medium quantities. They may be more difficult to obtain and have a higher level of risk.

Bottleneck items are typically considered to be critical to the organisation's operations, and the organisation may be heavily reliant on a few key suppliers for these items. As a result, it is important for the organisation to carefully manage the procurement and risk associated with these items. This may involve identifying alternative sources of supply, negotiating longer-term contracts with suppliers, or implementing inventory management strategies to mitigate the risks associated with obtaining these items.

The organisation may also have less bargaining power with suppliers of bottleneck items, as it may be less able to switch to alternative sources of supply due to the high volume of these items that it purchases. This may make it more difficult for the organisation to negotiate favourable prices or terms for these items.

The following questions can guide your organisation to identify bottleneck items in its procurement portfolio:

- What are the items that have a high rating on the organisation's risk footprint?
- What is the quantity of these items that the organisation purchases?
- How readily available are these items on the market?
- How many suppliers are available in the industry with capacity to supply these items?
- What is the level of risk associated with obtaining these items (e.g., are there any potential shortages or price fluctuations)?
- How much bargaining power does the organisation have with suppliers of these items?
- How important are these items to the organisation's operations?

- Can the organisation easily switch to alternative suppliers if necessary?

Non-critical items: These are items that have a low impact on the organisation's profitability and are purchased in small quantities. They are readily available and have low levels of risk.

Non-critical items are typically considered to be less important to the organisation's operations and may be more readily available on the market. As a result, the organisation may have more bargaining power with suppliers of these items, which can be used to negotiate favourable prices or terms.

Managing non-critical items effectively can help the organisation to reduce costs and streamline its procurement process. This may involve seeking out lower-cost suppliers, standardising on certain products, or implementing inventory management strategies to optimise the procurement of these items.

Here are some questions that an organisation might ask to identify non-critical items in its procurement portfolio:

- What are the items that have a low impact on the organisation's profitability?
- What is the quantity of these items that the organisation purchases?
- How readily available are these items on the market?
- What is the level of risk associated with obtaining these items (e.g., are there any potential shortages or price fluctuations)?
- How much bargaining power does the organisation have with suppliers of these items?
- How important are these items to the organisation's operations?
- Can the organisation easily switch to alternative suppliers if necessary?

Strategic items: These are items that have a high impact on the organisation's profitability and are purchased in large quantities. They may be more difficult to obtain and have a higher level of risk. Strategic items are typically considered to be critical to the organisation's operations, and the organisation may be heavily reliant on a few key suppliers for these items. As a result, it is important for the organisation to carefully manage the procurement and risk associated with these items. This may involve negotiating long-term contracts with suppliers, developing contingency plans in case of supply disruptions, or investing in in-house production capabilities.

The organisation may also have less bargaining power with suppliers of strategic items, as it may be less able to switch to alternative sources of supply due to the critical nature of these items. This may make it more difficult for the organisation to negotiate favourable prices or terms for these items.

Here are some questions that an organisation might ask to identify strategic items in its procurement portfolio:

- What are the items that have a high impact on the organisation's profitability?
- What is the quantity of these items that the organisation purchases?
- How readily available are these items on the market?
- What is the level of risk associated with obtaining these items (e.g., are there any potential shortages or price fluctuations)?
- How much bargaining power does the organisation have with suppliers of these items?
- How important are these items to the organisation's operations?
- Can the organisation easily switch to alternative suppliers if necessary?

The Kraljic matrix can help an organisation to identify the importance of different items in its procurement portfolio and to develop strategies for managing them. For example, an organisation may choose to focus on reducing the risk of obtaining strategic items, or it may choose to negotiate better prices for leverage items to increase profitability.

Risk Management/Mitigation

Risk footprint is a term used to describe the total amount of risk that a business is exposed to across all areas of its operations. In the procurement context, risk footprint can refer to the risks associated with sourcing goods and services from external suppliers. These risks may include financial risks, as well as operational risks, such as the risk of supply chain disruption or delays.

Risk management analysis is the process of identifying, evaluating, and prioritising risks to develop strategies to mitigate or eliminate them. In the procurement context, risk management analysis may involve:

Identifying risks: This involves identifying all the potential risks that a business may face when sourcing goods and services from external suppliers. This may include risks related to the supplier's financial stability, the quality of the goods or services, or the reliability of the supply chain.

Evaluating risks: Once risks have been identified, the next step is to evaluate them to prioritise which ones need to be addressed first. This may involve assessing the likelihood and impact of each risk, as well as the potential consequences if the risk were to materialise.

Mitigating risks: Once risks have been identified and evaluated, the next step is to develop strategies to mitigate or eliminate them. This may involve implementing controls or procedures to minimise the likelihood of a risk occurring or developing contingency plans to manage the consequences if a risk does occur.

Overall, risk footprint and risk management analysis are important concepts in the procurement context, as they help businesses to identify and manage the risks associated with sourcing goods and services from external suppliers. By understanding and addressing these risks, businesses can reduce the likelihood of disruptions or other negative impacts on their operations.

The risk management/mitigation exercise led by procurement is usually conducted annually. All key business leaders are invited into a workshop where they itemise all probable risks they foresee in their areas (as it affects the supply chain) and the financial impact they estimate if those risks were to materialise. These risks are then populated on a risk footprint/matrix to determine the biggest risks faced by the supply chain. Risk mitigation plans are then developed for the team to work on for the period.

The real value of conducting the workshop is to highlight the risks, but more importantly, to develop clear action plans to mitigate those identified as critical. This may involve developing alternative sources of supply, exploring in-house production of certain materials/services, evaluating backwards or forward integration options, a change in technology, skills acquisition/upgrade, tightening existing agreements with suppliers, and other ideas that reduce the impact of the risk or eliminate it completely.

In the sourcing strategy, the category manager will be required to develop a risk footprint/mitigation plan for the recommended buying approach. This would mean incorporating elements of the general risk management plan and doing a deep dive into the category to identify specific risks that may arise because of implementing the sourcing strategy. I recommend having a smaller workshop with category owners from the business units and any other experts to discuss a mitigation plan for any risks you identify from the exercise. This plan will form part of the document you will be sharing with business leaders for their approval. It will show that you are aware of scenarios that could possibly hinder the execution of your strategy and that you are working with the responsible stakeholders to mitigate those risks.

Sourcing Plan

The sourcing plan document is the equivalent of a project management plan for procurement. It is a task-based program for the execution of a sourcing strategy. It includes details such as the types of goods and services needed, the budget allocated for procurement, the timeline for the procurement process, and the evaluation criteria for selecting suppliers. A sourcing plan can also be used to guide the negotiation process, including setting out the terms and conditions of the contract and ensuring that the agreement aligns with the business's needs and goals.

Depending on the complexity of the items to be sourced, there are different variants of the sourcing plan. Here is an example of a procurement sourcing plan:

Title: Procurement Sourcing Plan for XYZ Company

Objective: To identify and select reliable suppliers for the procurement of goods and services needed by XYZ Company in a cost-effective and timely manner.

Scope: This procurement sourcing plan covers the procurement of goods and services required by XYZ company for the next 12 months.

Budget: The budget allocated for procurement is $XXX.

Timeline: The procurement process will begin on January 1st and will be completed by March 31st.

Procurement steps with timelines and individuals responsible for execution or implementation.

Identify the goods and services needed by XYZ Company.

Develop a request for proposal (RFP) and send it to potential suppliers.

Review proposals and shortlist suppliers based on their qualifications, experience, and pricing.

Conduct reference checks and site visits for the shortlisted suppliers.

Evaluate and compare the proposals received from the shortlisted suppliers based on the evaluation criteria.

Select the supplier that best meets the needs of XYZ Company and negotiate the terms of the contract.

Award the contract to the selected supplier and finalise the procurement process.

Evaluation criteria:

Quality of goods and services offered

Price of goods and services

Delivery time

Payment terms

Past performance of the supplier

This is just an example of a procurement sourcing plan. The specifics of the plan may vary depending on the needs of the business and the procurement process.

Sourcing Plan vs. Sourcing Strategy

The table above shows you the distinction between a plan and a strategy. In actual usage, a sourcing plan is developed as part of a sourcing strategy and should not stand alone. While the strategy guides the general buying approach for a three to five-year period, the sourcing plan specifies the actual buying activities for the transactional aspects of the process. Everything we have discussed up till now:

Business Needs

Linking

Industry Analysis

Supplier Analysis

Economic Analysis

Krailjc Model/Portfolio Analysis

SWOT Analysis, etc.,

are all pieces of strategy work that need to be done for each category to determine the principles and direction that procurement will follow. They provide the context and underlying information that feed into the sourcing plan. The level of rigour and detail will depend on the complexity of the category in question, but a sourcing plan should follow a strategy; otherwise, the procurement function just runs RFQs which, in my opinion, is an entry-level task and can be done by any procurement software.

We will now proceed to discuss two main elements of the sourcing plan – competitive bidding and negotiations.

Competitive Bidding: Maximising Value for Your Organisation

Competitive bidding is a process used to obtain quotes or proposals from multiple suppliers to identify the most suitable supplier for a particular goods or services requirement. Competitive bidding is typically used when a business needs to purchase goods or services that are important to its operations and wants to ensure that it gets the best value for its money.

Do you need to conduct a competitive bid for every spend item?

The answer is NO, you do not have to run a competitive bid for every procurement spend.

The bandwagon belief which has fuelled much of the mediocre knowledge in procurement is the 'three quote' myth. This methodology assumes that receiving price submissions from three suppliers and selecting the lowest of the three guarantees the 'best value'.

This is quite misleading and has encouraged some laziness and unprofessional behaviour among practitioners in the industry.

A little research reveals that the practice is prevalent in public sector procurement because it tries to create transparency in the use of taxpayer funds. The requirement is also for a 'minimum of three quotations'. What you find in practice, however, is that many of us have made it a gold standard for ethical procurement. At a very basic level of procurement knowledge, this makes sense; but as we begin to grow and deepen our understanding of markets and the categories we manage, a change in mindset is required.

Skills required to determine if CB is the right approach.

To determine if competitive bidding is the right approach to managing a spend category, you would require the skills and data we discussed earlier:

Supplier Analysis

Who are the suppliers in the industry? What are their capabilities? What is their perception of you as the buyer?

The insistence of leaders on the three-quote requirement has led to certain fraudulent practices such as supplier collusion (where suppliers agree on who gets the business each time) or employees generating quotations from unofficial sources to quickly meet defined service level agreements and turnaround times.

If your three-quote standard is not backed by industry information, I suggest you take a comprehensive look at your processes and work from a defined sourcing strategy.

Do a Kraljic portfolio analysis (strategic and bottleneck items may not have viable alternatives) – the typical work-around for a situation where three quotations cannot be obtained is to seek exceptional approval for 'violating' the policy.

Industry Analysis

Use the Five Forces model to understand where the 'power' lies and what you can leverage. If you receive a requisition and your first action is to search for suppliers you can send it to, you are doing it wrong. This is because a procurement process that is initiated by an RFx is already on the back foot and will never deliver value to the business. An industry analysis provides the context for the buying decision and should frame how the category should be approached. I wrote earlier that a doctor cannot prescribe medicine for symptoms he/she is yet to understand.

Competitive Analysis

What are your competitors doing? How are they approaching that spend category? Who are they buying from? Are they 'in-sourcing'?

Many years ago, I learnt that 'copying' best practices is one of the most competitive things you can do to succeed and have the edge in business. If your competitors have found a way to be successful in one area, you will do well to re-apply those ideas and not seek to invest in something new.

Linking

What are your business needs? What are the best solutions in the industry? How can you marry these? Your business units do not always share their 'real' challenges with you. They send you requests based on what they think will solve their problems. If you are the expert, as you should be, you will stay on top of innovations in the category and help them with robust solutions that meet their needs.

Leveraging

Are there any levers you can pull to make the most economically viable decision for your company? Are there opportunities you can take advantage of? Your broad knowledge of the business can sometimes allow you to take advantage of projects in more than one business unit or leverage on vendor solutions or relationships to drive value. As procurement, we are the only ones who can do this within the organisation.

You will note that the output of these exercises are sections in the sourcing strategy and buttress the need to use this almost-forgotten tool to demonstrate our professionalism and expertise.

Skills required to execute the competitive bidding process and evaluate the proposals.

Policy Application

A keen grasp of your procurement policies and procedures is required to conduct effective competitive bids. This is one area where it is so easy to run afoul of the process. When auditors show up to check compliance violations, they usually find multiple cases where procurement did not strictly follow its own process in this area especially. Because this is something we do the most often, it is easy to find instances where people unwittingly cut corners or do not toe the line.

Economic Analysis

There are cases where the company loses money or the bottom line is negatively impacted despite strict adherence to the competitive bidding process and multiple quotations and negotiations. This is where good economic analysis exposes holes in an otherwise 'low price' submission from vendors. 'Prices' do not tell all of the story as you must consider 'cost' and its implications on your operations. We will take a brief look at the concept of total cost at the end of the next section.

Understanding the Competitive Bidding Process

Review of business needs

We have discussed this in detail, and the expectation is that procurement professionals understand the needs of the business before proceeding to conduct a competitive bid. Everything from the strategic objectives of the company as cascaded to the business units and how that drives category management should guide these decisions.

Pre-RFx planning.

The efforts to ensure that the RFx output achieves the set objectives is covered in this section.

Evaluation criteria

'If you don't know where you're going, any road will take you there'.

Just like teachers prepare a marking scheme before setting examination questions, it is required that we prepare a set of criteria by which we will measure submissions from vendors. The defined parameters will be determined by the nature of the item and complexity of the transaction. An example of evaluation criteria elements is listed below:

Evaluation Criteria Elements

Experience: general capability of the supplier in the required area of expertise as evidenced by quality and quantity of work done to date.

Ability of the service provider to meet time deadlines: as evidenced by previous/existing client feedback and referrals.

Geographical needs: where the deliverables require presence in certain locations and is evidenced by infrastructure or partnership agreements in the required region(s).

Quality of the work in line with defined standards: evidenced by certificates of completion that meet set standards.

Ability of the service provider to provide necessary maintenance and assistance: evidence of post-delivery support set-up.

Local content: as guided by regulatory policies, some types of work in certain industries mandate the participation of indigenous vendors and suppliers who meet this requirement.

Cost of ineligible products and services: where some value add is built into the proposal, you should encourage vendors to highlight this so you can evaluate and score appropriately.

Project management expertise: this is relevant for work that requires extended implementation times. Look for previous project management deliveries within reasonable deadlines.

Management capability: the experience and track record of their management team, usually evidenced by known names within the industry who have successfully navigated difficult phases of growth.

Personnel qualifications: when a team is assigned to your project, you should request for resumes of experienced people with industry-standard qualifications.

Environmental objectives: evidence of an ECG agenda and a commitment to sustainability.

Experience with your organisation: you may specify this criterion where the work to be done requires some familiarity and experience with your organisation, especially where it involves the continuation of an existing project or unique resources.

Experience with similar organisations: to compensate for the absence of the previous criteria, you can request for evidence of work done with similar organisations (size, geography, technology, etc.) in your industry.

Cost of transition: with a change in technology, people, or major processes, request for an estimated transition cost, including timelines and resources required.

Technical expertise: usually created by the business unit, this criterion covers every measurable parameter that the solution will provide. It should be as detailed as possible and within acceptable industry standards.

Completeness of solution: pay attention to vendor proposals that do not go all the way to achieving your objectives. Be sure to request for evidence of how far the solution goes to meet your needs.

Reliability: how much maintenance would be required? How many breakdowns and support requests? Define these in the proposed SLA.

Integration with current infrastructure: some solutions do not work well together. Request for evidence of compatibility and ease of integration with whatever investments you have already and ensure additional costs and efforts are highlighted.

There are other criteria which you can include; the above are just a list of the most frequent ones. In using evaluation criteria, I propose the following guidelines.

Evaluation Criteria Guidelines

1. Develop, review, agree, and approve evaluation criteria before the competitive process begins.

2. Disclose the evaluation methodology, criteria and weightings, and the process to be used in assessing submissions, and the process for resolving a 'tied score' to all participating suppliers.

3. Issue a formal addendum to the RFx documents if you need to alter evaluation criteria.

4. DO NOT change evaluation criteria after the competition closes.

5. Criteria must not discriminate or be designed to create an advantage to a specific supplier.

6. Describe the short-listing process, including any minimum rated score requirements.

7. Describe the role and weighting of reference checks, oral presentations, product demonstrations.

8. Include the price/cost evaluation methodology, including the use of scenarios in the price calculation.

9. Three types of evaluation components.

***Mandatory requirements:** Failure to meet a mandatory requirement suspends further evaluation. Mandatory criteria should be kept to a minimum to ensure that no bid is unnecessarily disqualified.

Rated requirements: Documents may establish a minimum score for rated requirements. Bidders failing to meet this minimum would be eliminated from further consideration.

Price/cost: Particular attention must be paid to apply the maximum justifiable weighting to price/cost. Evaluation of price/cost should be undertaken after the completion of the mandatory and rated requirements.

*A note on mandatory requirements

You can define mandatory requirements or 'killer' criteria for specific requirements that disqualify incompetent vendors from the process, e.g., proof of Insurance or other relevant certifications. Only use them when they can withstand a legal challenge, as you don't want to be accused of influencing the procurement process.

Competitive Bidding – RFx types

'To the unskilled procurement employee, any reduction in a quoted price is value'.

Now we come to the most common tasks that many in our profession find themselves doing on a day-to-day basis – running RFx's. It was my intention to ignore this aspect of our work because it really is mundane and will soon be taken over by eProcurement platforms. In the context of future procurement, managing RFx's by themselves is entry-level, administrative, and not value-adding, especially when the objective is to reduce price.

To accurately determine right price, we need to understand cost structure. What are the cost elements of the supplier? What factors influence those costs, and how many of those factors are under their control?

Then we must do detailed calculations on life cycle costs or total cost of ownership (TCO). Acquisition costs (initial costs, transport costs, installation/commissioning costs, initial cost of spares, training costs); operation and maintenance costs (supervision, operator wages/salaries, energy costs, cost of materials used, insurance, servicing costs, wear and tear of spares, storage costs, maintenance of materials, depreciation); and lastly, disposal costs (including environmental impact and sustainability requirements).

The price at which an item is procured is important because it is quite visible at the point of purchase, but hidden costs can rubbish all your hard work if you do not consider them in your evaluation of value.

Value is often arrived at through collaborative exercises with your stakeholder. Procurement cannot define value exclusively.

If your internal customer places other business priorities above price, you must pull other levers in that transaction to deliver value.

However, I understand that we are at different levels of maturity, and several organisations are still dealing with the rudiments of the vast field of procurement: I have therefore included some guiding principles of the RFx process and how to manage them to drive value. The point to note is this: when an RFx is conducted as an outcome of a sourcing strategy, the results are significant and sustainable.

SOURCING FACTOR CONDITIONS	RFI	RFQ	RFB/IFB/IFT	RFP
Definable or Available Specifications or Requirements	Known and unknown	Known off-the-shelf goods and standard services	Known goods and services	Unknown detail, providing the what and why
Availability of Supplier Capability or Competitive Supplier Base	Known & unknown; depends on preferred or approved supplier lists	Known, usually qualified supplier list	Known & unknown, depends on preferred or approved supplier lists	Known, if RFI has been used
User or Internal Customer Collaboration	Encouraged by early purchasing involvement	Completed, off the shelf goods or standard type services	Usually completed	Required through early purchasing interaction
Level of Supplier Collaboration or Commercially Attractive	Encouraged by early supplier or vendor involvement	Completed since it is commercially attractive	Completed since it is commercially attractive	Required through supplier and vendor value proposition analysis
Need for Detailed Pricing Information	No, but standard pricing acceptable	Yes, based on trade custom/practice	Yes, based on your bid/tender guidelines	Yes or no, according to RFP format
Potential Savings Opportunities	Low potential	Low potential, but possibly negotiable	It depends if sealed bid or subject to BAFO	Very high, depending on spend category
Inherent Sourcing Risk	Low risk	Low to medium risk	Medium risk, more so if sole source	High risk

Source: https://www.purchasing-procurement-center.com/image-files/when-to-use-rfi-rfq-rfp-template.jpg

Request for information (RFI)

When you do not know enough about the items to be purchased, and you have some time, you can conduct an RFI. It's a market research type RFx where you request that suppliers provide you relevant and up-to-date information about the product or service. In an RFI, there is no obligation to place business after the exercise, but vendors are fully aware that you might have plans, so they are usually eager to share general information to guide you.

Request for quotation (RFQ)

This is the most common form of RFx where specifications are clearly defined, suppliers are known, and the objective is to award business to the lowest priced, technically compliant submission. I recommend sending a table with a list of categories to be priced for e.g., technical items, non-technical items, services, other costs, etc. This simplifies the process of evaluating vendor offers because you can see an itemised breakdown of what each offer is vs. the others.

An informal invitation to submit a quotation for requirements of relatively low monetary value. Prices and other commercial terms and conditions are requested, and an award is usually made to the lowest priced, technically compliant offer.

Invitation for bid (IFB)

Used to solicit bids from vendors or contractors for a specific project or service. It typically includes detailed specifications and requirements for the project or service, as well as instructions for submitting a bid.

Request for proposal (RFP)

The RFP seeks innovation and expertise from the vendors to implement ideas from the business unit. It differs from the RFQ in that the proposed budget is significant, and the project duration is extensive. A format for drafting RFPs is proposed below:

RFP structure

- Introduction

This is an overview of the RFP and the organisation issuing it, including contact information for the organisation and a brief description of the project or service being requested.

- Background

This section provides more detailed information about the organisation issuing the RFP and the project or service being requested, including any relevant history or context.

- Objectives

Here you outline the specific goals and objectives of the project or service being requested.

- Scope of Work

This section provides a detailed description of the work that needs to be done, including any specific tasks, deliverables, and timelines.

- Requirements

Are there any specific requirements that the organisation issuing the RFP has for the project or service, including technical specifications, compliance standards, and any other constraints?

- Evaluation Criteria

Outlines how the organisation issuing the RFP will evaluate and select a vendor or contractor, including the criteria that will be used and the weighting of each criterion.

- Submission Requirements

Provides instructions for how vendors or contractors should submit their proposal, including any required format, documentation, or certifications.

- Timeline

Provides a timeline for the RFP process, including key dates such as the deadline for submissions and the date when a vendor or contractor will be selected.

- Appendices

This section contains any additional information, such as diagrams, sample forms, or reference materials.

There are other types of RFx which are used for specific types of transactions, but they are just variants of the above.

RFx evaluation/bid clarity

When suppliers send in submissions in response to an RFP, the procurement and technical teams begin the process of going through loads of data and text to make sense of the proposals. Depending on the complexity of the purchase, this piece of work can take a while. If you defined the evaluation criteria properly and set up a pricing structure, you will only be tasked with understanding the innovative solutions offered by the vendors. Look out for the following:

When reviewing bid/proposal submissions from suppliers, it's important to thoroughly analyse the data.

- Gain a comprehensive understanding of market background data, including the industry dynamics that influence the prices you've received.

- Ensure that you're comparing 'apples to apples' and don't make any assumptions.

- Evaluate the submissions in their entirety, not just the price. Not everything offered may be of value, so review each aspect carefully.

- Be aware of the costs associated with qualifying and changing suppliers. If you're considering a change, determine the total costs of replacement and transition.

- Consider the value of innovation and what you're willing to trade for it. Which suppliers are introducing newer and simpler initiatives, and can you accurately assess the costs?

Have a plan B in place and know your backup options in case the primary option doesn't work.

Other considerations

- Note price validity or set yours in the RFP.
- Respect proprietary information – Use nondisclosure agreements.
- Don't share prices or technical information.
- These records may be required for legal proceedings.

Successful Negotiations

'Becoming a good negotiator is like learning to drive; you become better at it by doing it.'

I intended to omit this section entirely, but I can already read the questions that I will be forced to answer if I don't include a chapter on this most famous of all procurement topics.

'How can you write a book on procurement without a chapter on negotiations'?

'Isn't this a major part of the work you do in procurement'?

'Many people in procurement need this skill!'

When colleagues are asked to suggest training topics, the most frequently mentioned capability gap is negotiations.

You can read books about negotiation, you can watch videos, and understand all the principles. When you are faced with a tough opponent, the dynamics change so quickly that you may not remember the appropriate reaction to counter different tactics.

As with any other skill, negotiation skills are honed through knowledge, experience, and years of practice; the more you do it, the better you become at doing it.

Definition

'Negotiation is a deliberative process between two or more actors that seek a solution to a common issue or who are bartering over an item of value. Negotiation skills include the range of negotiation techniques negotiators employ to create value and claim value in their deal-making business negotiations and beyond. Negotiation skills can help you make deals, solve problems, manage conflicts, and build relationships as well as preserve relationships. Negotiation skills can be learned with conscious effort and should be practised once learned'.

Negotiation Skills Archives - PON - Program on Negotiation at Harvard Law School. (n.d.).

'Negotiation is an interactive process of discussions with the goal of influencing the behaviour of others to reach a satisfactory agreement and to build long term, competitively advantageous relationships'.

A few things to note about the definition above:

It is an interactive process: it usually involves more than one person communicating with each other to determine needs, options, etc.

It involves discussions: you are more likely to have the edge when you plan for these discussions. The better-prepared party is usually the more successful.

Influencing behaviour: what you want out of the exercise is to get the other party to behave a certain way without feeling manipulated or controlled.

Satisfactory agreement: the levels of satisfaction do not have to be equal, but they do have to meet each other's needs. Bear in mind that people will only do things that are in their interest, except, of course if they are forced.

Long-term, competitively advantageous relationships: this is consistent with the supply chain vision. As much as we strive for competitive advantage, we must always think beyond short-term results.

Now each party will have motivators that drive their positions on the issues.

Motivators: these are underlying corporate and personal feelings, desires, or needs that lie beneath e.g., one party's bonus or company's margin is tied to achieving a certain price or volume.

Positions: these are the numbers or specific conditions, terms, or offers that are put on the table e.g., $40 per kg, or $1.20 per km.

Issues: these are areas of interest in the negotiations e.g., price, length of contract, warranty terms, volume, etc. Issues are the items being disputed or around which agreements need to be reached.

Negotiators sometimes get stuck on the positions without understanding the issues. Really good negotiators focus on the motivators that drive the positions.

Negotiation – Planning

Here is a checklist that I think you will find useful as a planning guide for negotiations. It includes the following elements:

Is a BATNA in place?
At what stage is the professional relationship?
Are you aware of any tradeables?
Are you aware of the budget?
Are you aware of possible concessions?
Can the buyer afford to walk away?
Can the specification be amended?
Does the buyer have the required authority?
Does the supplier's representative have the required authority?
Have KPIs and SLAs been reviewed (if appropriate)?
How has the supplier performed (if established relationship)?

How important is the contract to supplier?
Is the negotiation a team or sole process?
Is the specification performance/conformance?
Is there a time limit for the negotiation?
Are the 'must haves' known?
Has market research been conducted?
What approach will be used?
What are the exchange rates?
What is the minimum/maximum order quantities?
What is an acceptable lead time?
What type of pricing mechanism is preferable?
What volumes are required?

If you can answer most of the questions above, you are mostly ready for the discussion. You do not need to have all the answers in every case; you only need to go into the negotiation with a clear picture of what you know and what you don't.

Negotiation – Strategy & Tactics

The outcome of the industry analysis, supplier analysis, and SWOT are useful sources of information that help you develop a negotiation strategy. You will also include your negotiation tactics in the sourcing strategy if that is the choice the data leads you to.

The negotiation strategy is the fundamental framework for the negotiation. Your organisation's strengths, for instance, can be leveraged while you take advantage of opportunities available to you, considering that the other party will be exploiting any weakness they can find. Your strategy should show a clear path to success so it receives alignment internally.

Your tactics will contain the operational details and specific approaches to optimise your potential. Details such as location, who should attend from each side, timing, seating arrangement, what to push for, concessions, etc. To succeed, negotiators must consider alternative tactics and counter-tactics the other party may use. The only way to know this beforehand is to do role-plays. In other words, think about the issues, interests, goals, priorities, likely strategies, and tactics for both sides. A colleague can act as you while you take on the role of the supplier. This will provoke you to think deeply and gain insight into how the other party may approach the issue. Consider the following negotiation tactics:

Paraphrase: Restating what your counterpart says using words that convey your understanding. This helps clarify the message.

Inquire: Ask open-ended questions and listen actively so you can understand the underlying motivations for their positions.

Acknowledge: Acknowledge what is said and what is not. If you detect feelings, bring them up so they can be addressed, and the conversation can move towards a resolution.

Find out if the barriers to agreement are tactical and/or interpersonal: When you're close to a good deal for both parties but find that are stuck, the issue may be something personal or cultural.

When a deal can't be reached because of the way it's designed or because the setup is flawed: Look at other ways you can create value for both sides and find out if you're dealing with the right parties, issues, or interests.

Negotiations – BATNA

BATNA is an acronym for best alternative to a negotiated agreement, or, more simply put, your plan B (backup plan). It is the position at which you are willing to walk away from the negotiation table and explore other options if you fail to reach an agreement at the bargaining table with your counterpart.

An evaluation of your BATNA is critical if you are to establish the threshold at which you will reject an offer. Effective negotiators determine their BATNAs before talks begin.

BATNA Tips

- Have more than one BATNA – Have a backup plan for your backup plan, just in case.

- Protect a weak BATNA – If your backup plan is a weak one, do not reveal it in negotiations, as it places you in a difficult position.

- Your BATNA might be stronger than it looks – Sometimes, the other party will deliberately make your options look weaker than they are. Don't yield to this.

- Find out what their BATNA is – If you can, find out what the other party's walkaway position is.

- Determine when a BATNA has two levels – In certain situations, the person sitting across the table from you may have other motivations aside from the objectives defined by his/her organisation. If you can determine this, it may put you in a stronger position.

- Do not feel entitled – a BATNA that is too good tends to undermine the current negotiation process as it almost becomes unnecessary to engage.

Negotiations – Role-Plays

For practice with negotiations, I recommend the Hackerstar negotiation video. It is the most complete demonstration of all the elements of negotiations that we can teach. Watch the video to see the principles and styles at work, and then download role-play case studies from https://www.pon.harvard.edu/shop/category/case-studies-articles/ for your team to use in practice.

Negotiations – Power and Leverage

To be effective in negotiations, you need to have power and leverage. Power comes from:

- Planning – you know what you need, what, and where you are flexible.
- Alternatives – you have options.
- Reward/punish – you have some control over the outcome for the other party.
- Internal Alignment – you are the decision-maker.
- Confidence – you demonstrate you know what you are talking about so others believe you.
- Persona/charisma – others like and trust you.
- Normative/social proof – your requests fall within the social and industry norms established.
- Competition – your offer is competitive within the industry.
- Legitimacy – your requests are real and valid.
- Time – you don't have to rush your decision, OR the other party needs a deal done quickly.
- Patience – you can wait out the other party.
- Trust/reputation – people believe and listen to you.

- Knowledge – you know what you are discussing so the other party cannot give you incomplete information.

Leverage would mostly come from knowledge. And this brings us to the next chapter.

Total Life Cycle Costs: Understanding the True Costs of Procurement

Life cycle costing (LCC) is a method of analysing the total cost of a product or service over its entire life cycle. This includes the initial cost of procurement as well as any ongoing costs such as maintenance, repairs, and disposal. By considering these costs over the life of the product or service, organisations can make more-informed decisions about their procurement choices, with a focus on value for money. LCC can be used to compare different products or services, identify cost-saving opportunities, and evaluate the long-term financial impact of procurement decisions.

Total cost of ownership (TCO – the more commonly used term in procurement), is a method of evaluating the financial impact of a product or service throughout its entire lifecycle. It includes all the costs associated with acquiring, using, and disposing of a product or service rather than just the initial purchase price. The TCO calculation typically includes costs such as:

- Acquisition costs, including the purchase price, freight, and installation costs.

- Operating costs, including energy consumption, maintenance, and repairs.

- Disposal costs, including any costs associated with recycling or disposing of the product.

By considering these costs over the entire lifecycle of the product or service, organisations can make more informed decisions about their procurement choices and optimise their overall spend. TCO is a widely used method for procurement professionals to evaluate the long-term value of products and services and to identify cost-saving opportunities. It can also be used to compare different products or services to determine which one is the most cost-effective over the long term.

A clearer way of determining costs during negotiations with suppliers is to itemise their offerings into obvious and hidden costs.

Obvious Costs

Obvious costs are those costs that are easily identifiable and quantifiable, such as the purchase price of a product or service, freight and handling charges, and taxes. These costs are typically included in the initial purchase price and can be easily tracked and reported.

Purchase price: The cost of buying the product or service from the supplier.

Freight and handling charges: The cost of shipping the product or service from the supplier to the organisation.

Taxes: Any taxes or duties that are applicable to the purchase of the product or service.

Insurance costs: The cost of insuring the product or service during transport or storage.

Financing costs: The costs associated with borrowing money to purchase the product or service, such as interest or loan fees.

Customisation costs: The costs of customising the product or service to meet the organisation's specific needs.

Warranty costs: The cost of any warranty or maintenance agreements associated with the product or service.

Employee costs: The cost of employee time spent on the procurement process, such as research, negotiation, and processing payments.

Legal and compliance costs: The cost of ensuring compliance with regulations and laws, such as certifications, permits, or licenses.

Travel and accommodation costs: The cost of travel and accommodation for employees visiting suppliers or suppliers visiting for repairs and maintenance.

Obvious costs can vary depending on the type of product or service and the industry.

Hidden Costs

Hidden costs, on the other hand, are costs that are not immediately obvious and may not be included in the initial purchase price. These costs can include things like installation costs, training costs, maintenance costs, and disposal costs. Hidden costs can be more difficult to identify and quantify, and they may not be included in the initial purchase price.

These are some examples of hidden costs:

Installation/deployment costs: The cost of installing or setting up the product or service, including the cost of any necessary equipment or labour, costs of configuring space, transporting, installing, setting up, integrating with other assets, and outside services, especially when these are not handled by the supplier.

Training costs: The cost of training employees on how to use the product or service, including any necessary training materials or travel expenses.

Maintenance costs: The cost of maintaining and repairing the product or service, including the cost of replacement parts or labour.

Disposal costs: The cost of disposing of the product or service, including the cost of recycling or disposing of any hazardous materials.

Depreciation expense tax savings: Refer to the reduction in a business's tax liability that results from claiming depreciation expenses. When a business claims depreciation expenses on its tax return, it reduces its taxable income, which in turn reduces the amount of tax it owes to the government.

Operating costs: The cost of energy consumed by the product or service, such as electricity or fuel or human labour required to operate the equipment.

Storage costs: The cost of storing the product or service, such as warehouse or storage fees.

Shipping costs: The cost of shipping the product or service to and from the supplier or to different locations.

Insurance costs: The cost of insuring the product or service during transport or storage.

Downtime costs: The cost of lost productivity or revenue due to equipment downtime.

Legal and compliance costs: The cost of ensuring compliance with regulations and laws, such as certifications, permits, or licenses.

Upgrade/enhancement costs, reconfiguration costs:

Change management costs: Cost of user orientation, user training, workflow/process change design and implementation.

Infrastructure support costs: Costs brought by the acquisition for heating/cooling, lighting, or IT support.

Environmental impact costs: Cost of waste disposal/clean up, pollution control, or the costs of environmental impact compliance reporting.

Security costs: Physical security, security additions for a building, including new locks, secure entry doors, closed circuit television, and security guard services; electronic security (security software applications or systems, offsite data backup, disaster recovery services, etc.).

Financing costs: Loan interest and loan origination fees.

It's important to note that the list of hidden costs can vary depending on the type of product or service and the industry. Also, some of the above examples can be considered as obvious costs in some cases.

The concept of obvious and hidden costs is important in procurement because it helps organisations to understand the full cost of a product or service. By considering both obvious and hidden costs, organisations can make more informed decisions about their procurement choices and optimise their overall spend. Additionally, considering hidden costs in procurement can help organisations to identify cost savings opportunities and to avoid unexpected expenses.

<u>NOTE!</u> The time to identify and calculate hidden costs is during the RFx process as it provides leverage for negotiations. If you only find out after you have placed orders or taken delivery of the equipment or service, you have incurred additional costs for the company. Sit down with your colleagues in finance and request for a general ledger total of all the costs that are charged to the P&L for the stuff you buy. This way, you know if your efforts are adding value or not.

Writing a Recommendation for Approval: Presenting Your Case Effectively

This section covers the headers a typical recommendation from procurement should have. In my experience, we do a lot of re-work because of the way we present our requests for approval. If you have spent valuable time doing a sourcing strategy and running an RFx, why would you want all that wasted because you did not take the time to write a proper recommendation for approval? I suggest you include the following headers in your document.

Start with your recommended action.

Begin by stating what you want, be clear and concise, save the rationale for later, and explain if there is 'money left on the table' or any opportunity cost (this is the cost of going with your recommendation instead of the alternatives).

Include a brief background.

Describe the existing market conditions, your business trends, the impact of any initiatives, and your history with these suppliers.

State your conclusions.

The impact on suppliers; where an incumbent is losing business, for instance, describe the recommended award, relative to suppliers' overall spend with your company and the potential impact on the suppliers' overall business.

Detail the impact of your recommendation on your company.

Show the impact on savings, cash, other key measures (use TCO!). Are qualifications needed (training, supplier audits, etc.), are there any unique benefits or risks, any supplier relationship implications, is there an impact on other business units, etc.?

Include some general discussion.

The 'why' or rationale of your recommendation (use lots of data). Market forces and cost evolution explain how this allocation meets the business needs and overall strategic direction, show how the allocation aligns with your sourcing strategy, highlight any key benefits, identify, and explain risks (and backup plans).

End your recommendation with next steps.

State what happens next, be clear on who will do what and by when, get alignment and approval, refer to your delegation of decision-makers.

Keep all your records intact!

Engaging in Award Discussions with Suppliers

After you have received approval for your recommended action, it is proper to have an award discussion with the recommended supplier(s). It is always advised to speak with the successful supplier first (to be sure they are still interested in the business) and use the others as a backup if discussions fail at this stage (very unlikely if you have been thorough and kept them updated through the process). I suggest you do the following:

Award Discussion Guidelines:

- Communicate outcome & enable execution – provide whatever is required from your side to help them begin work; advance payments, site/access permissions, purchase orders, contracts, etc.

- Explain rationale for results – tell them 'why' they were successful.

- Encourage winners and losers – send a message to ALL suppliers. Thank the unsuccessful for participating and assure them of an ongoing relationship regardless of the immediate results.

Why Do We Need to Do This?

- All suppliers (winners and losers) need to know what the outcome is.

- Everybody needs to understand what to do next. For example, if a new supplier needs to be qualified or contracts need to be initiated.

- ALL suppliers deserve an explanation of HOW we arrived at the outcome.

- The successful supplier(s) needs to continue to provide the best value; the unsuccessful need to be encouraged to continue and try again.

- This promotes ongoing competition and lets them know that they always have a chance in future RFx and sets the 'tone' for the next time – they will feel valued and be willing to participate in later processes.

After the Award Discussion

Summarise discussions with bidders in meeting minutes, send thank you letters to everyone, keep your internal stakeholders informed, and celebrate successes.

Effective Contract Management: Ensuring Compliance and Performance

After the award of business, there is the small matter of purchase orders and contracts to be handled.

Types of Purchase Orders

There are several types of purchase orders:

Blanket purchase order: This type of purchase order is used for repetitive purchases from a specific supplier. It sets a maximum spending limit and a specific time frame for the purchases to be made.

Contract purchase order: Used when a buyer enters a contract with a supplier for a specific product or service. It includes details such as delivery dates, payment terms, and any specific requirements.

Standing purchase order: Used for ongoing, regular purchases from a supplier. It remains in effect until it is cancelled or expires.

Planned purchase order: Used for future purchases that are planned. It helps to ensure that materials and products will be available when needed.

Drop-ship purchase order: This type of purchase order is used when a supplier ships products directly to the customer, bypassing the buyer's warehouse.

Stockless purchase order: This type of purchase order is used when the supplier doesn't keep stock of the items and produces the item when ordered.

Contract management is the process of managing and organising the terms and conditions of a contract to ensure that all parties involved are meeting their obligations and that the contract is being carried out as intended. This can involve a variety of activities, including negotiating terms, monitoring performance, and resolving disputes.

Contract management refers to reviews, analyses, and other measures that help keep contracts on track throughout the contract's lifecycle. An effective contract management process means that your contracts are located in a centralised location, organised, secure, and can be reported on easily. People tasked with managing contracts need to be able to locate files quickly, understand how a contract is serving the organisation, and identify strategies to help the business operate more effectively.

Types of Procurement Contracts

Procurement contracts are agreements between a buyer and a seller for the acquisition of goods, services, or works. There are several types of procurement contracts, including:

Fixed-price contracts: The price for the goods or services is agreed upon in advance and does not change, regardless of the actual cost incurred by the supplier.

Cost-reimbursement contracts: The supplier is reimbursed for their actual costs, plus a fee for profit.

Time-and-materials contracts: The supplier is paid for the materials used and the time spent on the project.

Unit-price contracts: The supplier is paid a pre-agreed price per unit of goods or services provided.

Indefinite-delivery contracts: The buyer agrees to purchase an unspecified quantity of goods or services over a specified period.

Performance-based contracts: The supplier is paid based on their performance rather than the completion of specific tasks.

Framework contract: A long-term agreement between a buyer and a supplier for the supply of goods, services, or works for a specific purpose and specific period.

Partnership contract: A contract where both the buyer and the supplier work together to achieve common goals.

Contract Terms

Common contract terms are clauses or provisions that are typically included in most contracts. Some of the most common contract terms include:

Offer and acceptance: Defines the terms of the offer made by one party and the acceptance of that offer by the other party, creating a binding agreement.

Consideration: This is the exchange of something of value, such as money or services, between the parties in the contract.

Performance and obligations: This refers to the specific tasks or actions that each party is required to perform under the contract.

Timeframe: The start and end date of the contract and any deadlines for performance or completion.

Termination: Defines the conditions under which the contract can be terminated by either party before the completion of the contract.

Confidentiality: The terms under which the parties will keep the information shared within the contract confidential.

Dispute resolution: The process that will be followed in the event of a dispute between the parties.

Governing law and jurisdiction: Provide guidance as to the laws that govern the contract and the jurisdiction where any disputes will be resolved.

Indemnification: The liability of one party to the other in the event of any loss or damage caused by the former's actions.

Force majeure: Any event(s) that would excuse the parties from performance under the contract due to unforeseen circumstances.

Contract Management Systems

Contract administration and contract management are processes that organisations use to oversee and manage their agreements with external parties, such as vendors, suppliers, and service providers. The goal of these processes is to ensure that the terms of the contract are met and that the organisation is getting the best value for its investment.

Contract administration is the process of monitoring the performance of a contract and ensuring that it is being executed in accordance with its terms and conditions. This includes tasks such as tracking deliverables, monitoring payment schedules, and addressing any issues that arise during the contract.

Contract management, on the other hand, is a broader process that encompasses the entire lifecycle of a contract, from the initial negotiation and drafting stages to contract execution, monitoring, and closeout. This process includes tasks such as identifying potential vendors, developing requests for proposals, evaluating bids, negotiating terms, and creating and executing the final contract.

Contract management systems, also known as contract management software, are designed to automate and streamline these processes. They provide tools for creating, storing, and tracking contracts, as well as features such as workflow management, document management, and automated reminders and alerts. These systems can also include reporting and analytics capabilities to help organisations gain insights into their contract performance and identify areas for improvement.

There are several key elements of contract management:

Contract negotiation: The process of negotiating the terms and conditions of a contract with a supplier or other party. This includes defining the scope of work, setting pricing and payment terms, and establishing performance metrics and timelines.

Contract execution: The process of finalising and executing the contract, including the signatures of both parties and the delivery of any required documentation.

Contract administration: The ongoing management of the contract, including monitoring compliance with the terms and conditions, managing invoicing and payments, and addressing any disputes or issues that may arise.

Performance monitoring: The process of monitoring the supplier's performance against the terms and conditions of the contract, including quality and delivery metrics.

Contract closeout: The process of closing out the contract at the end of its term, including the collection of final payments, the resolution of any outstanding issues, and the archiving of contract documents.

Risk management: The process of identifying and managing risks associated with the contract, such as the risk of non-performance or disputes, and implementing measures to mitigate or avoid those risks.

Compliance: The process of ensuring that the contract complies with all relevant laws, regulations, and organisational policies.

Communication and collaboration: The process of maintaining open lines of communication and collaboration with the supplier throughout the contract term to ensure that the contract is executed smoothly and efficiently.

Reporting: The process of generating and distributing reports on the performance of the contract, including financial and operational data.

Contract Management Software

I strongly recommend the use of a contract management software because of the following benefits:

- Managing documents electronically, including storing, searching, and retrieving contracts, can save time as it eliminates the need for manual filing and searching.

- The use of technology in creating and negotiating contracts, such as the ability to draft, edit, and make changes through redlining, can reduce errors and increase efficiency.

- Electronic signature features allow you to get contracts signed in minutes, reducing the time needed to execute new agreements.

- Tracking and reporting, which enables monitoring of expiration and renewal dates, compliance with terms, and financial performance in relation to the contract's terms, can provide better visibility and control over the contract's lifecycle.

- Managing the process through technology, such as routing them for review, approval, and execution by the relevant parties, can streamline the workflow and increase efficiency.

- Linking contract management software with other systems, such as accounting and procurement, can enable data consistency and automate contract-related tasks, making the process more efficient and effective.

A contract management software serves as a centralised repository where all an organisation's contracts are stored, ensuring that all users have access to the correct and up-to-date information. This eliminates the confusion and errors that can arise from having multiple copies or versions of a contract circulating and ensure that everyone is working off the same agreement.

With contract management software, businesses can easily access and search all their contracts, clauses, and keywords, rather than having to manually search through scattered contracts in various desks, shared drives, and filing cabinets. This leads to improved visibility and understanding of the contract portfolio.

Contract management software helps minimise risk by providing tools for monitoring contract dates and deadlines, such as setting reminders for critical dates and deadlines, which can help prevent missed automatic renewals or contract deliverables.

It enables stakeholders to access reports and insights based on any contract metadata, which can be used to improve visibility and understanding of the contract portfolio. This allows for better monitoring of contract adherence and performance not just by the legal team but also by department heads and leadership teams.

Contract reporting provides an effective way to evaluate past agreements and identify patterns by isolating underperforming contracts and analysing the commonalities. This helps in understanding what went wrong and making changes in future contracts to avoid repeating the same mistakes.

Contract management software is beneficial as it saves a significant amount of time, allowing you to focus on more important tasks. The manual process of managing contracts can be tedious, but most software features are created with the goal of saving time.

Artificial intelligence features automatically identify and tag key pieces of information in your contracts, potentially saving you and your team from spending hundreds of hours manually entering these details.

Permission-based user roles give administrators the option of assigning varying levels of access to different groups and users, enabling your colleagues to find answers to their contract-related questions without requiring your time and attention.

Implementing dedicated contract management software streamlines the contract management process and enables key members of the legal department to spend less time on tedious contract management tasks and more time on strategic, high-value initiatives.

Contract administration and contract management represent two different stages of the contracting process, covering the periods before and after a contract is signed and put into effect. To ensure all your organisation's agreements are created, executed, organised, monitored, and optimised according to company standards, it's important to have strong contract administration and contract management processes and systems in place.

Some are also able to flag new contracts for clauses that may have generated disputes in the past and offer suggested edits and corrections. If your company can invest in a decent contract management platform, you will enjoy these benefits and more.

When Is a Contract Required?

Depending on the value and risk of the transactions of your business, this is a grey area. There are some criteria I have used, and I think it can be adapted and used today.

	Equipment/Hardware	Services
Time	Longer than XX months	Longer than XX months
	OR	OR
Purchase Amount	Greater than XX amount in local currency	Greater than XX amount in local currency

Regardless of the purchase amount or time conditions in the table, a written contract should be established if one or more of these risk factors exist:

- Hazardous material or environmental risk potentially involved.
- Hazardous activity (e.g., lifting or unloading).
- The company supplies materials to supplier.
- Potential public relations issues exist.
- Development project confidentiality or proprietary property issues are involved.

- An unusual risk, cost, or possibility of dispute exists due to non-standard or undefined requirements, undeveloped specifications, or rush schedule.
- Supply assurance is a significant risk.

Supplier Performance Management: Evaluating and Improving Supplier Performance

Supplier performance management is the process of evaluating and improving the performance of a business's suppliers to ensure that they meet the business's needs and expectations. Effective supplier performance management can help a business to identify and address any issues or challenges with its suppliers and ensure that it is able to access the goods and services it needs in a timely and cost-effective manner.

To conduct supplier performance management effectively, you would need to:

Define performance expectations: This may include expectations related to the quality of the goods or services, delivery times, pricing, and any other requirements or expectations that are relevant to the business.

Establish performance metrics: Used to measure and evaluate the performance of suppliers. These metrics may include measures such as on-time delivery, quality of goods or services, and cost efficiency.

Monitor supplier performance: This may involve collecting and analysing data on supplier performance and identifying any areas where improvements are needed.

Communicate and collaborate: Effective supplier performance management also involves regular communication and collaboration with suppliers to address any issues or challenges that may arise. This involves working with suppliers to develop and implement improvement plans or identifying alternative solutions if necessary.

Review and revise: It is important to regularly review and revise the supplier performance management process to ensure that it is effective and aligned with the business's needs and goals, review the performance metrics that are used, and adjust the process as needed to better meet the business's needs.

Supplier Performance Management Measures

A supplier performance scorecard is a tool that organisations can use to measure and evaluate the performance of their suppliers. Below are examples of measures that can be used to measure supplier performance:

Quality: This measures the supplier's ability to meet quality requirements and standards and can include metrics such as the number of defects, the number of customer complaints, and the percentage of products that pass inspection.

Delivery: The supplier's ability to deliver products or services on time, including metrics such as the percentage of on-time deliveries, the number of late deliveries, and the percentage of orders that are shipped complete.

Cost: Measures the supplier's ability to deliver products or services at a competitive price, such as the unit cost of products, the total cost of goods, and the percentage of cost savings achieved through the supplier.

Responsiveness: Measures the supplier's ability to respond to customer needs and requests. This can include metrics such as the average response time for customer inquiries, the percentage of customer requests that are fulfilled within a specific timeframe, and the percentage of customer complaints that are resolved within a specific timeframe.

Innovation: Measures the supplier's ability to provide innovative products or services. This can include metrics such as the number of new products or services introduced, the percentage of sales from new products or services, and the number of patents filed by the supplier.

Compliance: Measures the supplier's ability to comply with legal and regulatory requirements. This can include metrics such as the number of safety incidents, the number of environmental incidents, and the percentage of audits that pass without non-compliances.

Relationship: Measures the supplier's ability to maintain a positive working relationship with the organisation. This can include metrics such as the number of face-to-face meetings, the number of joint projects completed, and the percentage of supplier evaluations that are positive.

Supplier Performance Management Scorecard

The scorecard should include a weighted system to indicate the relative importance of each category and a way to calculate the overall supplier performance score. It should also include a way to track supplier performance over time and identify areas for improvement.

This is an example of a table that could be used to assign weights to the categories in the supplier performance scorecard. You can include as many measures as are required and modify the weights to suit your objective.

Measure	Weight	Rating	Score
Quality	25%		
Delivery	20%		
Cost	15%		
Responsiveness	15%		
Innovation	10%		
Compliance	10%		
Relationship	5%		

You can adjust the weight according to the importance of each category to your organisation. The sum of the weights should be 100%.

The rating should be multiplied by the weight to achieve a score. I advise that this assessment be done by the user teams and reviewed by procurement for fairness. Do not wait until the end of the contract period to perform this assessment; it should be done periodically so that one snapshot in supplier performance does not determine the continuation or termination of the contract. It's also important that the scorecard is reviewed and updated regularly to ensure that it remains relevant and meaningful and that the weighting system reflects the current priorities of the organisation.

Measuring Procurement Performance

Procurement managers play a critical role in the success of the organisation by ensuring that the right goods and services are acquired at the right price and delivered on time. Measuring their performance is essential to ensure that they are delivering value to the organisation. By tracking key performance metrics such as cost savings, supplier performance, inventory management, contract compliance, on-time delivery, quality assurance, risk management, procurement process efficiency, and stakeholder satisfaction, organisations can identify areas for improvement and optimise their procurement function.

The effectiveness of procurement processes and performance can significantly impact the success of an organisation. It is, therefore, essential to evaluate the efficiency and effectiveness of procurement processes, identify areas for improvement, and make informed decisions about procurement strategies.

Effective measurement of procurement performance requires the collection and analysis of relevant data from procurement processes and systems. Procurement data analytics tools and technologies can help organisations gain insights, identify areas of improvement, and make informed decisions.

This chapter will provide a comprehensive overview of the key metrics and approaches to measuring procurement performance. It will cover the importance of the different metrics used to evaluate the challenges involved and best practices for measuring procurement performance.

The Importance of Measuring Performance

Measuring procurement performance is critical to the success of any organisation, regardless of its size or industry. Procurement is responsible for acquiring goods and services from suppliers to support organisational operations, and the effectiveness of procurement processes and performance can significantly impact business operations.

One of the primary reasons for measuring performance is to identify areas for improvement so that organisations can gain insights into the effectiveness of their procurement processes, identify areas for improvement, and implement strategies to optimise procurement activities. This can help organisations reduce costs, increase efficiency, and enhance the quality of goods and services acquired.

Another reason why this is crucial is that it enables organisations to make data-driven decisions about procurement strategies. By collecting and analysing procurement data, organisations can identify trends, opportunities, and potential risks and make informed decisions.

Measuring procurement performance also helps organisations ensure compliance with legal and ethical standards. Procurement is subject to various regulatory requirements and guidelines, such as those related to environmental sustainability, labour practices, and anti-corruption. Measuring compliance metrics can help organisations ensure adherence to these standards and mitigate legal and reputational risks.

In addition, measuring procurement performance can help organisations manage procurement-related risks. By identifying potential risks related to suppliers, supply chain disruptions, or business continuity, organisations can implement strategies to mitigate these risks and ensure the continuity of operations.

Metrics used to Evaluate Performance

The below table lists and describes metrics used in evaluating performance in procurement.

Performance Metric	Description
Cost Savings	Measure of the procurement manager's ability to negotiate better pricing and terms with suppliers. Can be measured as a percentage of the total spend or as a dollar value.
Cost Avoidance	Measure of the procurement manager's ability to identify and mitigate potential cost increases in the supply chain. Can be measured as a percentage of the total spend or as a dollar value.
Supplier Performance	Measure of the procurement manager's ability to manage supplier relationships and ensure they meet performance expectations. Can be measured using a supplier performance scorecard or other similar tools.
Inventory Management	Measure of the procurement manager's ability to optimise inventory levels and minimise stock-outs. Can be measured as a percentage of stock-outs or as a dollar value of inventory carrying costs.
Contract Compliance	Measure of the procurement manager's ability to ensure that suppliers adhere to contract terms and conditions. Can be measured by tracking the number of contract disputes and resolutions.
On-Time Delivery	Measure of the procurement manager's ability to ensure that purchased goods and services are delivered on time. Can be measured by tracking the percentage of on-time deliveries.
Quality Assurance	Measure of the procurement manager's ability to ensure that purchased goods and services meet quality standards. Can be measured using a quality assurance scorecard or other similar tools.
Risk Management	Measure of the procurement manager's ability to identify and mitigate supply chain risks. Can be measured by tracking the number of supply chain disruptions and resolutions.
Procurement Process Efficiency	Measure of the procurement manager's ability to optimise procurement processes and reduce cycle times. Can be measured by tracking the procurement cycle time or the percentage of purchase orders processed without errors.
Stakeholder Satisfaction	Measure of the procurement manager's ability to meet the needs of internal stakeholders such as business units and end-users. Can be measured using a stakeholder satisfaction survey or other similar tools.

Challenges involved in Measuring Performance

There are challenges with capturing and reporting accurate performance metrics:

- **Data Collection and Analysis Challenges:** This is due to the complexity of procurement processes and systems. Procurement data may be scattered across different systems, making it difficult to gather comprehensive and accurate data. Incomplete or inaccurate data can also make it challenging to measure performance meaningfully.

- **Lack of Alignment with Organisational Goals and Objectives:** Metrics that do not align with organisational goals and objectives can lead to meaningless measurement, and these cannot drive organisational success.

- **Difficulty in Measuring Intangible Benefits:** Some procurement benefits, such as increased supplier collaboration or stakeholder satisfaction, are difficult to quantify. Measuring such benefits requires the use of subjective measures that may lack objectivity, making it challenging to meaningfully measure procurement performance.

- **Inconsistency in Data Collection and Analysis:** This can make it difficult to compare performance metrics and identify areas for improvement.

- **Limited Resources and Expertise:** Limited resources, such as staff and technology, can make it challenging to collect, analyse and report on procurement performance data. A lack of expertise in data analytics can also limit an organisation's ability to accurately measure this.

- **Complexity of Procurement Processes:** Procurement processes can be complex and can involve multiple stakeholders, including suppliers, finance, legal, and other departments. Measuring performance accurately, therefore, requires the collaboration and support of multiple teams, making it a challenging process.

Best Practices for Measuring Procurement Performance

I recommend that organisations should follow best practices that include the following:

- **Define Clear Goals and Objectives:** Organisations should establish clear goals and objectives that align with their goals. These goals and objectives should be specific, measurable, achievable, relevant, and time-bound (SMART).

- **Select Appropriate Metrics:** Metrics based on goals and objectives is critical to meaningful measurement. Organisations should select metrics that accurately measure performance, align with goals and objectives, and are relevant to the procurement function's purpose.

- **Establish a Data Collection and Analysis Process:** This is critical to accurately measuring procurement performance. Organisations should ensure that data is collected consistently and accurately, and that data analysis is comprehensive, providing insights into performance.

- **Monitor Performance Regularly and Report Results to Stakeholders:** Monitoring procurement performance regularly and reporting results to stakeholders is critical to drive accountability and continuous improvement. Reporting results to stakeholders will help demonstrate the value of procurement, improve decision-making, and promote collaboration across departments.

- **Continuously Improve Procurement Processes Based on Performance Metrics:** Using performance metrics to identify areas for improvement and continuously improving procurement processes is essential to drive organisational success. Doing this can help organisations optimise procurement strategies, reduce costs, increase efficiency, and enhance the quality of goods and services acquired.

- **Leverage Technology:** Adopting data analytics tools and technologies can help organisations gain insights into procurement performance, improve data accuracy, and optimise procurement strategies. Technology can automate data collection and analysis, enabling procurement teams to focus on strategic decision-making.

Balanced Scorecard

A balanced scorecard is a performance management tool that can be used to measure the effectiveness of a procurement manager. It typically consists of four key elements that reflect a balanced view of the procurement manager's performance: financial, customer, internal processes, and learning and growth. Below is a discussion of each of these elements and their relevance to a procurement manager's performance:

Financial: The financial element of a balanced scorecard measures the procurement manager's impact on the organisation's financial performance. This includes metrics such as cost savings, cost avoidance, and return on investment (ROI). A procurement manager who can negotiate better pricing and terms with suppliers can help to reduce costs and increase profitability for the organisation. Additionally, a procurement manager who can identify and mitigate potential cost increases in the supply chain can help to avoid unnecessary expenses and improve the organisation's financial performance.

Customer: The customer element of a balanced scorecard measures the procurement manager's impact on customer satisfaction. This includes metrics such as on-time delivery, quality assurance, and stakeholder satisfaction. A procurement manager who can ensure that purchased goods and services are delivered on time and meet quality standards can help to improve customer satisfaction and build strong relationships with stakeholders.

Internal Processes: The internal processes element of a balanced scorecard measures the procurement manager's impact on internal operations. This includes metrics such as procurement process efficiency, contract compliance, and inventory management. A procurement manager who can optimise procurement processes and reduce cycle times can help to improve efficiency and minimise errors. Additionally, a procurement manager who can ensure that suppliers adhere to contract terms and conditions can help to reduce risk and improve operational performance.

Learning and Growth: The learning and growth element of a balanced scorecard measures the procurement manager's impact on employee development and learning. This includes metrics such as training and development, employee satisfaction, and supplier performance management. A procurement manager who can foster a culture of learning and growth can help to improve employee satisfaction and retention. Additionally, a procurement manager who can effectively manage supplier relationships and ensure that suppliers meet performance expectations can help to build a strong and reliable supply chain.

By measuring performance across these four dimensions, organisations can ensure that their procurement managers are delivering value to the organisation and driving continuous improvement.

Embracing Future Supply Chain Technology

The future of supply chain technology is likely to involve a greater use of advanced technologies such as artificial intelligence (AI), machine learning (ML), the internet of things (IoT), blockchain, and robotics. These technologies have the potential to improve supply chain efficiency, increase visibility, and reduce costs.

In today's fast-paced business environment, organisations must embrace the latest technologies to stay ahead of the competition. Supply chain management is no exception. The integration of advanced technologies such as artificial intelligence, machine learning, internet of things (IoT), blockchain, robotics, 3D printing, procurement analytics, and procurement automation has revolutionised the supply chain management process. In this chapter, we will explore the key future technologies that can help organisations optimise their supply chain management.

AI-powered systems can analyse large amounts of data to identify patterns and predict future demand, enabling companies to optimise their supply chain operations. IoT-enabled devices can be used to track the movement of goods and assets in real time, allowing companies to have greater visibility into their supply chain and make more informed decisions. Blockchain technology can be used to create secure, tamper-proof digital records of transactions, making it useful for tracking the movement of goods and ensuring the authenticity of products. Robotics and automation can be used to improve the efficiency of warehouse and distribution operations and increase productivity in manufacturing. 3D printing allows for on-demand production, which reduces the need for inventory and allows for more customisation. Procurement analytics refers to the use of data, statistical and quantitative analysis, explanatory and predictive models, and fact-based management to drive decision-making in the procurement process, while procurement automation is the use of technology to automate repetitive and manual tasks in the procurement process, such as purchase order creation, invoice processing, and supplier management.

Let us look at these technologies in detail and how they are being applied in supply chain management.

Artificial Intelligence

Artificial intelligence (AI) has rapidly emerged as a promising technology in the field of supply chain management. AI applications in supply chain management can help organisations optimise their operations, increase efficiency, and reduce costs. Artificial intelligence (AI) is a field of computer science that focuses on creating machines and software that can perform tasks that would typically require human intelligence, such as perception, reasoning, and learning. The goal of AI is to build intelligent machines that can understand complex problems, learn from experience, and make decisions based on data.

AI has been a topic of interest for many years, with researchers and developers working to create intelligent machines since the 1950s. Over the years, advancements in computer hardware, software, and algorithms have allowed AI to progress rapidly. Today, AI is used in a wide range of applications, including self-driving cars, virtual assistants, and medical diagnosis.

The origins of AI can be traced back to the Dartmouth Conference in 1956, where a group of researchers gathered to discuss the possibility of creating intelligent machines. At the time, the field was in its early stages, and the researchers had ambitious goals but limited resources.

In the 1960s and 1970s, AI research focused on building expert systems which were designed to mimic human decision-making processes. Expert systems were used in a wide range of applications, including medical diagnosis, financial analysis, and engineering design.

In the 1980s and 1990s, AI research shifted towards machine learning, which allowed machines to learn from data without being explicitly programmed. This led to the development of neural networks, which are computing systems modelled after the structure of the human brain. Neural networks are used in many AI applications, including speech recognition and image classification.

In the 21st century, AI research has continued to advance rapidly, with the development of deep learning, which involves training large neural networks on vast amounts of data. This has led to breakthroughs in many areas, including natural language processing, computer vision, and robotics.

There are three main types of AI: narrow or weak AI, general or strong AI, and artificial superintelligence.

Narrow or weak AI refers to AI that is designed to perform a specific task or set of tasks, such as facial recognition or natural language processing. Narrow AI is the most common form of AI and is used in many applications, including virtual assistants, chatbots, and recommendation systems.

General or strong AI refers to AI that can perform any intellectual task that a human can do. General AI is the goal of AI research and would require machines to have a wide range of intellectual abilities, including reasoning, problem-solving, and creativity.

Artificial superintelligence is AI that is more intelligent than any human. This is a theoretical concept that has not yet been achieved, but some researchers believe that it could be possible in the future.

AI is being used in many applications in healthcare, including medical diagnosis, drug discovery, and personalised medicine. AI algorithms can analyse medical images, such as X-rays and MRIs, to detect abnormalities and diagnose diseases. AI is also being used to develop new drugs and therapies that can be personalised to individual patients.

In many applications in finance, including fraud detection, risk management, and trading, AI algorithms can analyse large amounts of financial data in real time, identifying patterns and anomalies that can help detect fraud and prevent financial losses. AI is also being used to develop trading algorithms that can make trades based on market data and trends.

Well-known applications of AI are its use in transportation, including self-driving cars, traffic management, and logistics optimisation. AI algorithms can analyse traffic patterns, predict traffic congestion, and optimise transportation routes to reduce travel time and improve fuel efficiency.

In supply chain management, AI can be used in the following processes.

Demand forecasting: AI can analyse past sales data and market trends to predict future demand, helping companies optimise their inventory levels and reduce the risk of stockouts.

Inventory management: AI algorithms can monitor inventory levels in real time, predict demand, and automatically reorder products when necessary. This can help companies reduce excess inventory, improve cash flow, and prevent stockouts.

Logistics optimisation: AI can help companies optimise their shipping routes and transportation modes based on real-time data, reducing transportation costs, and improving delivery times.

Supplier management: AI can analyse supplier performance data, such as delivery times and quality of goods, to help companies make better supplier selection and negotiation decisions.

Warehouse optimisation: AI algorithms can optimise warehouse layouts, product placement, and picking paths to improve efficiency and reduce labour costs.

Quality control: AI can analyse product quality data in real time, identifying defects and predicting potential quality issues before they occur.

Sustainability: AI can help companies optimise their supply chains to reduce environmental impact, such as by optimising transportation routes to reduce emissions or identifying opportunities to use more sustainable materials.

One of the main challenges of AI is the potential loss of jobs as machines and software become more intelligent and can perform tasks that were previously performed by humans. This could lead to significant economic and social disruptions, particularly in industries that rely heavily on manual labour.

Another challenge is the potential for AI to be biased or discriminatory, particularly in applications such as hiring or lending, where decisions could be made based on factors such as race or gender. Ensuring that AI systems are fair and unbiased is a complex issue that requires careful consideration and ongoing monitoring.

There are also risks associated with the use of AI, including the potential for malicious actors to use AI for nefarious purposes, such as hacking or cyber-attacks. Ensuring the security and safety of AI systems is a critical issue that requires ongoing research and development.

Machine Learning

Machine learning (ML) is a subfield of artificial intelligence (AI) that focuses on creating algorithms and models that can learn and make predictions from data. ML has been rapidly gaining popularity in recent years due to its ability to process large amounts of data and make accurate predictions.

Machine learning is a type of AI that enables systems to learn and improve from experience without being explicitly programmed. ML algorithms use statistical techniques to analyse data and learn patterns that can be used to make predictions. The goal of machine learning is to create systems that can automatically improve their performance by learning from data.

There are three main types of machine learning: supervised learning, unsupervised learning, and reinforcement learning. In supervised learning, the system is trained on labelled data to learn a function that maps input to output. Unsupervised learning, on the other hand, involves training the system on unlabelled data to identify patterns and relationships in the data. Reinforcement learning is a type of learning where the system learns through trial and error by receiving feedback in the form of rewards or punishments.

There are several machine learning algorithms that can be used for different types of problems. Some of the popular algorithms include decision trees, random forests, support vector machines, k-nearest neighbours, and neural networks. These algorithms can be applied to various domains, such as healthcare, finance, and image recognition.

Machine learning has numerous applications in various fields, such as healthcare, finance, and marketing. In healthcare, machine learning is used to predict disease outcomes, identify risk factors, and improve patient care. In finance, ML is used to detect fraud, predict stock prices, and manage portfolios. In marketing, ML is used to personalise advertising, optimise pricing, and improve customer retention.

In supply chain, AI and ML can be used in various ways, such as:

Predictive analytics: AI and machine learning algorithms can analyse large amounts of data to identify patterns and predict future demand. This can help companies optimise their inventory levels, production schedules, and logistics operations.

Optimisation: Machine learning algorithms can be used to optimise supply chain processes such as routing, scheduling, and inventory management, reducing costs and improving efficiency.

Quality control: AI and machine learning algorithms can be used to monitor production processes and identify defects in real time, improving quality control and reducing the risk of defects.

Risk management: Machine learning algorithms can be used to analyse data from various sources to identify potential risks in the supply chain, such as natural disasters or geopolitical instability, and help companies develop mitigation strategies.

Autonomous vehicles and drones: AI and machine learning can be used to control the movement of autonomous vehicles and drones, which can be used for logistics and transportation in the supply chain.

AI and machine learning are still in early stages of being adopted in the supply chain, but they are expected to have a significant impact in the future. As more companies adopt these technologies, they will be able to make more-informed decisions, improve operational efficiency, and increase their agility in the face of rapidly changing market conditions.

Amazon has implemented machine learning to improve demand forecasting and inventory optimisation. The company has reduced inventory costs by over 20% and improved customer satisfaction.

DHL has implemented machine learning to improve logistics planning and routing. The company has reduced transportation costs by over 10% and improved on-time delivery rates.

Intel has implemented machine learning to improve quality control in its manufacturing operations. The company has reduced defect rates by over 50% and improved product quality.

Some of the challenges of ML include the quality and quantity of data, the interpretability of results, and the potential for bias in the algorithms. It is crucial to ensure that the data used for training ML algorithms are of high quality and free from biases.

ML has become an essential tool in modern technology, and its use continues to grow. ML algorithms can help to automate and improve decision-making processes in various domains, leading to more efficient and effective outcomes. However, as with any technology, it is essential to address the challenges and ensure that machine learning is used ethically and responsibly.

Internet of Things (IoT)

The internet of things (IoT) has emerged as a promising technology that can revolutionise the way supply chain management (SCM) is executed. IoT technologies can enable real-time monitoring of various stages in the supply chain, including production, inventory management, transportation, and delivery. This can result in increased efficiency, reduced costs, and enhanced customer satisfaction.

IoT is a network of physical objects, such as sensors, devices, and machines, connected to the internet and capable of communicating with each other. The key components of IoT include:

- Sensors and Devices: These are physical objects that capture data about their environment, such as temperature, humidity, location, and movement.
- Connectivity: This refers to the technologies used to connect the sensors and devices to the internet, such as Wi-Fi, Bluetooth, and cellular networks.
- Data Analytics: This involves processing the data generated by the sensors and devices to extract insights and make decisions.
- Cloud Computing: This involves storing the data generated by the sensors and devices on remote servers and accessing it from anywhere in the world.

IoT can be applied in various stages of the supply chain, as follows:

Production: IoT can be used to monitor the production process in real time and identify any inefficiencies or bottlenecks. For example, sensors can be placed on machines to track their performance and detect any malfunctions or maintenance requirements. This can help reduce downtime and increase productivity.

Real-time tracking: IoT-enabled devices can be used to track the movement of goods and assets in real time, allowing companies to have greater visibility into their supply chain and make more informed decisions.

Inventory management: IoT-enabled devices can be used to monitor inventory levels in real time, enabling companies to optimise their inventory and reduce the risk of stockouts.

Predictive maintenance: IoT-enabled devices can be used to monitor the condition of equipment and predict when maintenance is needed, reducing downtime, and improving efficiency.

Quality control: IoT-enabled devices can be used to monitor production processes and identify defects in real time, improving quality control and reducing the risk of defects.

Smart logistics: IoT-enabled devices can be used to optimise logistics operations, such as route planning, vehicle tracking, and cargo monitoring.

Coca-Cola is using IoT to monitor the performance of its vending machines in real time. The machines are equipped with sensors that track their inventory levels, temperature, and condition. This allows Coca-Cola to optimise its supply chain by restocking machines when they run low on inventory and identifying any maintenance requirements before they become a problem. This has resulted in reduced downtime and increased sales.

Walmart is also using IoT to track the location and movement of goods throughout its supply chain. The company has installed sensors on its trucks and trailers to monitor their location, speed, and condition. This allows Walmart to optimise its routing and scheduling of shipments and ensure that products are delivered on time and in good condition. This has resulted in reduced transportation costs and improved customer satisfaction.

As more organisations adopt IoT, we can expect to see further innovation and transformation in the supply chain management field.

Blockchain

Blockchain technology is still in the early stages of adoption in supply chain management, but it has the potential to improve transparency, security, and efficiency in the supply chain. As more companies adopt blockchain technology, it could become the backbone of a more secure and transparent supply chain, enabling companies to better manage their operations and build trust with their customers.

Blockchain is a distributed ledger technology that allows for secure, transparent, and immutable transactions between parties without the need for intermediaries. It is a decentralised digital ledger that records transactions across a network of computers. It uses cryptography to secure and validate transactions, making it difficult to tamper with or alter the recorded data.

The history of blockchain dates back to 2008 when an anonymous person or group of people known as Satoshi Nakamoto published a whitepaper titled "Bitcoin: A Peer-to-Peer Electronic Cash System". This paper introduced the concept of blockchain as a secure and decentralised method for recording and verifying transactions in a digital currency system. Since then, blockchain technology has been applied in a wide range of industries and has become a major area of research and development.

The current state of blockchain technology is characterised by the development of increasingly sophisticated blockchain platforms that offer a range of features and functionalities. These platforms include Bitcoin, Ethereum, and many others, each with its own unique strengths and weaknesses. Some of the most significant advances in blockchain technology in recent years include the development of smart contracts, which allow for the automated execution of contractual agreements, and the emergence of decentralised finance (DeFi) applications, which enable financial transactions to be conducted without the need for traditional financial intermediaries.

Blockchain technology has a wide range of applications, including in finance, supply chain management, healthcare, and voting systems. In finance, blockchain technology is being used to create digital currencies, such as Bitcoin and other cryptocurrencies, as well as to facilitate the transfer of assets and the execution of contracts. In supply chain management, blockchain technology is being used to track the movement of goods and ensure their authenticity and quality. In healthcare, blockchain technology is being used to create secure and transparent medical records, and in voting systems, blockchain technology is being used to create secure and tamper-proof voting systems.

Traceability: Blockchain can be used to create a tamper-proof digital record of all transactions in a supply chain. This allows companies to trace the movement of goods from the manufacturer to the end consumer, making it useful for tracking the authenticity of products and detecting counterfeit goods.

Smart contracts: Blockchain can be used to automate the execution of contracts, reducing the need for intermediaries and increasing the efficiency of supply chain operations.

Payment and settlement: Blockchain can be used to facilitate secure and fast payments, settlements, and financial transactions, reducing the cost and time of traditional payment methods.

Supply chain finance: Blockchain can be used to create a distributed platform for supply chain finance, which can facilitate access to funding for suppliers and manufacturers and improve working capital management.

Walmart has implemented blockchain technology to improve traceability in its food supply chain. The company has created a transparent and tamper-proof record of the movement of goods from suppliers to customers, which has helped to improve food safety and reduce the risk of counterfeit products.

Maersk has implemented blockchain technology to improve transparency and reduce fraud in its shipping operations. The company has created a transparent and auditable record of compliance with regulations such as labour and environmental standards, which has helped to improve accountability and reduce the risk of legal liability.

Everledger has implemented blockchain technology to create a transparent and tamper-proof record of the movement of diamonds from suppliers to customers. The company has created a secure and auditable record of the provenance of each diamond, which has helped to reduce the risk of counterfeit products and improve trust in the diamond industry.

Despite the many benefits of blockchain technology, it also presents several challenges. One of the most significant challenges is the scalability of blockchain platforms, as the current generation of blockchain platforms can only handle a limited number of transactions per second. Additionally, there are concerns about the security of blockchain platforms, as they are vulnerable to attacks from hackers and other malicious actors. Other challenges include the legal and regulatory implications of blockchain technology, as well as the need for interoperability between different blockchain platforms.

Blockchain technology has the potential to revolutionise many aspects of our lives, from finance to healthcare to supply chain management. While there are challenges associated with blockchain technology, the potential benefits are enormous, including increased efficiency, transparency, and security. As blockchain technology continues to evolve and mature, it is likely to play an increasingly important role in the future of supply chain management.

Robotics

Robotics is a rapidly growing field that involves the design, construction, and operation of robots. Robots are machines that can perform a variety of tasks, from manufacturing to performing surgery to exploring outer space.

The history of robotics dates to ancient times when inventors created mechanical devices to automate various tasks. However, the first modern robot was invented in 1954 by George Devol and Joseph Engelberger, who created the Unimate, a robotic arm used for industrial manufacturing. Since then, robotics technology has advanced rapidly, and robots have become increasingly sophisticated, capable of performing a wide range of tasks in various industries.

The current state of robotics is characterised by the development of increasingly intelligent and autonomous robots. These robots are equipped with sensors and algorithms that enable them to sense their environment, make decisions, and perform complex tasks without human intervention. Some of the most significant advances in robotics technology in recent years include the development of humanoid robots, which are designed to resemble and interact with humans, and the development of autonomous vehicles, which can drive themselves without human input.

Robotics has a wide range of applications, including manufacturing, healthcare, transportation, and space exploration. In manufacturing, robots are used to automate various tasks, such as assembling products, welding, and painting. In healthcare, robots are used to perform surgeries, assist with rehabilitation, and provide elderly care. In transportation, robots are used to drive autonomous vehicles, and in space exploration, robots are used to explore planets and perform scientific experiments.

In the context of supply chain management, robotics can be used in various ways, such as:

Automation of warehouse and distribution operations: Robotics technology can be used to automate the picking, packing, and shipping of goods in warehouses and distribution centres, increasing productivity and reducing labour costs.

Automation of manufacturing processes: Robotics can be used to automate repetitive tasks in manufacturing, such as assembly, welding, and painting, improving efficiency and reducing the risk of errors.

Transportation and logistics: Robotics technology can be used to control the movement of autonomous vehicles and drones, which can be used for logistics and transportation in the supply chain.

Inspection and monitoring: Robotics can be used to perform inspections and monitoring tasks in hazardous or hard-to-reach environments, such as inspecting pipelines, power plants, and mines.

Robotics technology is becoming more prevalent in the supply chain, and it is expected to play a bigger role in the future. Robotics can improve the efficiency and productivity of supply chain operations, reduce costs, and increase the accuracy of tasks.

Autonomous robots are robots that can operate without human intervention. These robots use sensors and other technologies to navigate and complete tasks.

Collaborative robots are robots that can work alongside humans. These robots are designed to be safe and easily programmable.

Mobile robots are robots that can move around freely in a facility. These robots are often used in warehousing and transportation.

Amazon has been a pioneer in the use of robotics in its fulfilment centres. The company has deployed thousands of robots in its warehouses to automate processes such as picking and packing. According to a report by Deutsche Bank, the use of robots has helped Amazon to reduce operating expenses by 20%.

DHL has implemented autonomous mobile robots in its warehouses to automate material handling processes. The robots are equipped with sensors and cameras to navigate and avoid obstacles. The use of robots has helped DHL to improve efficiency and accuracy in its warehouse operations.

JD.com, a Chinese e-commerce company, has implemented a fully automated warehouse that uses robots for picking, packing, and sorting. The warehouse can handle up to 200,000 orders per day with minimal human intervention. The use of robots has helped JD.com to improve efficiency and reduce labour costs.

Despite the many benefits of robotics technology, it also presents several challenges. One of the most significant challenges is the potential impact on employment, as robots are increasingly used to replace human workers. Additionally, there are concerns about the safety of autonomous robots and the potential for them to malfunction or cause harm to humans. Other challenges include the ethical implications of robots, such as the potential for robots to be used for warfare, as well as the high cost of developing and deploying robotics technology.

Robotics technology has come a long way since the invention of the Unimate in 1954. Today, robots are increasingly intelligent and autonomous, capable of performing complex tasks in a wide range of industries.

3D Printing

3D printing, also known as additive manufacturing, is a rapidly growing technology that enables the creation of complex three-dimensional objects using computer-aided design (CAD) software and various materials. This technology has revolutionised the manufacturing industry, enabling the creation of customised and intricate designs that were previously impossible to produce using traditional manufacturing techniques.

3D printing is a process that involves creating a digital model of an object using computer-aided design software and then using a 3D printer to transform that model into a physical object by adding material layer by layer. The process starts with creating a 3D model of the object that needs to be printed. This can be done using CAD software or by scanning an existing object using a 3D scanner. The 3D model is then sliced into a series of 2D cross-sections, which are sent to the 3D printer. The printer then uses a variety of materials, such as plastics, metals, or even organic materials, to build up the object layer by layer.

The applications of 3D printing are vast and varied. Some of the most common applications include rapid prototyping, product design and development, medical implants, dental crowns and bridges, aerospace and automotive parts, architectural models, and educational tools. 3D printing has also been used to create complex structures such as living tissue and organs, which have the potential to revolutionise the field of medicine.

In a supply chain, 3D printing will impact:

On-demand production: 3D printing allows for on-demand production, which reduces the need for inventory and allows for more customisation. This can help companies reduce their inventory costs and improve their responsiveness to changes in demand.

Rapid prototyping: 3D printing allows for rapid prototyping, which can speed up the product development process and reduce the time to market.

Local production: 3D printing enables companies to produce parts and products locally, which can reduce transportation costs and improve the efficiency of supply chain operations.

Tooling and fixtures: 3D printing can be used to create custom tooling and fixtures, which can improve the efficiency of manufacturing processes and reduce costs.

Spare parts: 3D printing allows for on-demand production of spare parts, which can reduce inventory costs, and General Electric (GE) has implemented 3D printing to create spare parts for its aviation business. The company has reduced lead times from months to days and reduced inventory costs by over 50%.

Adidas has implemented 3D printing to create customised shoes for customers. The company has reduced the time and cost of product development and improved customer satisfaction.

Ford has implemented 3D printing to create prototypes of new vehicle parts. The company has reduced the time and cost of product development and improved the quality of its products.

While 3D printing technology has many advantages, it also presents some challenges. One of the most significant challenges is the cost of 3D printers and the materials used in the printing process. Additionally, the speed of the printing process is still relatively slow compared to traditional manufacturing techniques, making it challenging to use 3D printing for mass production. Another challenge is the quality of the printed objects, which can be affected by factors such as the resolution of the printer and the quality of the materials used.

The technology is rapidly evolving, and its applications are expanding. As the cost of 3D printing continues to decrease and the speed and quality of the printing process continue to improve, we can expect to see 3D printing become more widely used in manufacturing and other industries. The potential benefits of 3D printing are enormous, including the ability to create complex and customised designs quickly and efficiently.

Procurement Analytics

Procurement analytics has become increasingly important in today's business environment. The digital age has given rise to a vast amount of data that organisations can use to gain insights into their procurement processes. Procurement analytics help organisations make data-driven decisions that can improve procurement efficiency, reduce costs, and improve supplier performance. By leveraging procurement analytics, organisations can:

- Optimise procurement processes.
- Reduce costs.

- Improve supplier performance.
- Enhance risk management.
- Enhance collaboration with suppliers.
- Improve decision-making.

There are three main categories of procurement analytics:

Descriptive analytics involves the analysis of historical data to gain insights into past procurement performance. Descriptive analytics helps organisations understand their procurement processes, identify areas for improvement, and monitor procurement KPIs such as spend analysis, supplier performance, and contract compliance. Predictive analytics uses statistical techniques and machine learning algorithms to analyse historical data and make predictions about future procurement performance. Predictive analytics helps organisations identify potential risks and opportunities, forecast demand, and optimise procurement processes. Prescriptive analytics uses advanced algorithms to suggest the best course of action based on the analysis of historical data. Prescriptive analytics helps organisations optimise procurement processes, reduce costs, and improve supplier performance.

Some applications of procurement analytics are in the following areas:

Spend analysis: This is the process of analysing an organisation's spend data to gain insights into its procurement processes. Spend analysis helps organisations identify areas of spend, analyse supplier performance, and identify cost-saving opportunities to gain insights into their procurement processes and make data-driven decisions that can improve procurement efficiency and reduce costs.

Supplier performance analytics: This involves the analysis of supplier data to gain insights into their performance. Supplier performance analytics helps organisations identify high-performing suppliers and address underperforming suppliers. This helps organisations improve collaboration with suppliers and enhance supplier performance.

Contract compliance analytics: Contract data is analysed to ensure that suppliers are complying with the terms of their contracts. Contract compliance analytics helps organisations identify non-compliant suppliers and take corrective action to reduce the risk of legal disputes.

Risk management analytics: This helps organisations identify potential risks such as supplier bankruptcies, supply chain disruptions, and regulatory compliance issues to proactively mitigate risks and reduce the impact of potential disruptions.

Pfizer, a leading pharmaceutical company, used spend analysis to identify areas of spend, analyse supplier performance, and identify cost-saving opportunities of $600 million. Procter & Gamble used predictive analytics to forecast demand, improve supplier performance, and reduce inventory costs by $2 billion. By leveraging prescriptive analytics, IBM was able to optimise procurement processes, reduce costs, and improve supplier performance.

To successfully implement procurement analytics, organisations need to develop a data strategy that outlines how they will collect, manage, and analyse procurement data. The data strategy should include data governance, data quality, and data integration. Advanced analytics tools such as machine learning, artificial intelligence, and natural language processing can help organisations identify patterns, trends, and anomalies in their procurement data that are not easily identifiable using traditional analytics tools. Collaboration with suppliers can help organisations gain insights into their suppliers' operations, improve communication, and enhance trust.

Monitoring key performance indicators of spend analysis, supplier performance, contract compliance, and risk management can help organisations identify areas for improvement and take corrective action.

Procurement Automation

Procurement automation refers to the use of technology to automate the various manual and repetitive tasks involved in the procurement process. It involves the use of software applications and tools that enable organisations to automate vendor selection, purchase order creation, invoice processing, and payment processing. The use of automation in procurement can help organisations to reduce manual effort, increase efficiency, and improve accuracy.

The use of procurement automation can offer several benefits to organisations, including:

Increased Efficiency: Employees can focus on more critical tasks, such as vendor management and strategic sourcing, instead of time-consuming and repetitive tasks, such as data entry and document processing.

Improved Accuracy: Manual procurement processes are often prone to errors, such as data entry errors, incorrect pricing, and inaccurate invoice processing. The use of procurement automation can help to reduce errors and improve accuracy, resulting in better financial management and cost savings.

Better Vendor Management: Procurement automation can help organisations to manage vendors more effectively by providing real-time data on vendor performance, contract compliance, and other metrics.

Improved Compliance: Organisations can comply with internal policies, as well as external regulations such as GDPR and HIPAA. Automated processes can ensure that data is handled securely and that all procurement activities are recorded and auditable.

Examples of procurement automation include:

Electronic purchase order (ePO) systems: These systems allow companies to create and track purchase orders electronically, reducing the need for manual intervention and increasing efficiency.

Electronic invoice processing (eInvoice) systems: These allow companies to process invoices electronically, reducing the need for manual data entry and increasing accuracy.

Supplier management systems: These systems allow companies to manage their suppliers electronically, including tracking supplier performance, managing contracts, and communicating with suppliers.

Spend analysis systems: These systems allow companies to analyse their spending patterns and identify areas of overspending or potential savings opportunities.

Source-to-pay systems: These systems automate the entire procurement process, from sourcing and supplier selection to purchase order creation and invoice processing.

Challenges that organisations must overcome to implement automation successfully include:

Integration with legacy systems: Many organisations have invested heavily in their existing procurement systems, and it can be challenging to replace or upgrade these systems. Integration can be complex, requiring coordination between IT teams and procurement teams, and may involve significant customisation and configuration.

Resistance to change: Some employees may be resistant to the changes brought about by automation, either because they are comfortable with existing processes or because they fear that automation will reduce their role or lead to job loss. Overcoming resistance to change can require clear communication, training, and education to help employees understand the benefits of automation and how it can support their work.

Data quality and standardisation: As mentioned earlier, data quality is critical to the success of procurement automation. However, many organisations struggle with data quality and standardisation, particularly if data is siloed across different departments or stored in different formats. Improving data quality and standardisation may require significant effort to clean up existing data, establish data governance policies, and train employees on how to enter data correctly.

Cost and return on investment: Automation can be expensive to implement, particularly if significant customisation or integration work is required. Organisations must weigh the cost of automation against the potential benefits, such as increased efficiency, cost savings, and improved supplier management. Calculating return on investment (ROI) can be challenging, particularly if the benefits of automation are difficult to quantify.

Final Thoughts and Reflections

Throughout this book, I have also emphasised the critical importance of effective procurement policies and processes, from developing comprehensive procurement policies and SOPs to crafting effective sourcing strategies and conducting successful negotiations. Effective contract management and supplier performance management are also critical components of successful procurement processes.

There are many books on the principles of procurement; however, I decided to add something a little different to the library of available material. I agonised through the 18 months or so of writing this book. I had many arguments with myself over what to include and what to leave out, how much detail to go into, which examples to share, and whether it would be worth it in the end. I have spent my career in the field, so I know what the day-to-day work life of a procurement professional looks like.

The procurement profession has come a long way, and it continues to evolve rapidly. From its early beginnings as a transactional function focused on cost savings, procurement has become a strategic function that drives value and innovation for organisations. Today, procurement professionals are expected to be business partners, change agents, and thought leaders who can navigate complex internal and external stakeholder environments, develop and execute sourcing strategies, and manage supplier relationships effectively.

Throughout this book, we have explored the many facets of procurement, from the fundamentals of procurement mastery to the intricacies of supplier performance management and the potential of emerging supply chain technologies. We have discussed the importance of building positive procurement reputations, adapting to changing needs, and nurturing procurement teams to drive growth and success.

This book has provided a comprehensive overview of the procurement profession, from its history and evolution to the skills, processes, and technologies required to succeed in today's dynamic business environment. We have explored the key concepts and techniques of procurement fundamentals, the importance of building positive relationships with stakeholders, the critical role of procurement policies and procedures, and the art of developing successful sourcing strategies.

One of the key themes that emerges throughout this book is the critical importance of effective communication, both within procurement teams and with external stakeholders. Procurement professionals must be able to navigate complex procurement politics, build strong relationships with suppliers and other stakeholders, and communicate effectively to present their case and secure approval for their procurement decisions.

We have also discussed the importance of understanding the true costs of procurement, the value of effective negotiations and contract management, and the critical role of supplier performance management. In addition, we have explored the impact of emerging technologies such as AI, machine learning, IoT, blockchain, robotics, 3D printing, and procurement analytics on the procurement function. This requires that we adapt to changing needs and embrace emerging technologies to drive efficiency and effectiveness in procurement processes. The rise of AI and machine learning, the internet of things, and blockchain technology have the potential to revolutionise procurement processes and drive significant changes and efficiency gains.

As we look to the future, we can expect the procurement profession to continue to evolve and transform in response to changing business and technological landscapes. Procurement professionals will need to stay abreast of these changes, continue to develop their skills and knowledge and embrace innovation and disruption to remain relevant and effective.

In a workshop I facilitated some years back, the participants laughed and scoffed at my suggestion that they schedule study time into their daily calendar. I understand why the idea seems idealistic, and I empathised with them at the time. However, think about the following questions:

How long do you want to continue firefighting?

Do you look forward to coming to work every day?

Is this it for you?

Is your daily work schedule the career you dreamed of?

Is this the best that you can give yourself?

I have written this book to inspire my colleagues and friends in the industry to be more and to believe that there can be a life of growth, productivity, and career fulfilment in procurement. We can do better than just treating RFx's and bargaining during negotiations. We can be experts and recognised business leaders; we can elevate this profession and ourselves to become the pool from which COOs, CFOs, and, yes, CEOs are selected.

If we develop ourselves and our teams, redesign our work to approach every business need from the standpoint of a sourcing strategy and manage our stakeholders to jointly drive business performance, we will be acting as business executives at our level and will have prepared ourselves for the C-Suite opportunity when it does come. This may not happen to everyone in their career, but I am following the universal principle to 'preach to many and peradventure, we might save some'.

Earlier in this book, I shared examples of CEOs who began their careers in our industry. My firm, unwavering belief is this: 'Of all the professions, the type of work we do prepares us best for business leadership. If a business is heavily dependent on supply chain management and logistics, a leader with a strong background in those areas may be particularly effective in a COO or CEO role. They will bring valuable expertise in areas such as cost control, risk management, and process improvement.

As I write this conclusion, many tech companies are laying off thousands of employees; however, Tim Cook, the Apple CEO (at the time of writing), has just taken a massive pay cut instead. He hopes to keep as many of his staff on payroll so they can keep making great products and leading the market. This is the mindset of a true supply chain professional; we make sacrifices so our people can keep going.

The question I usually get is this:

'With the kind of work we do, when will we have the time to invest in and develop ourselves'?

My answer is always the same:

'What do you want'?

If you have decided that the career you have presently and the work you do every day does not point you in the direction you want to go, then you should consider doing something different or doing things differently. We can whine about how much recognition we are not getting, how unreasonable our stakeholders are, and how we seem to be stuck at one level, but nothing will change if we don't approach our work from another perspective.

The framework in this book helped me navigate and build a career, and I have shared them with you, hoping that they shine a light on your path and lead you to taking a *seat at the table,* as you learn to efficiently manage yourself and the procurement function.

I hope that this book has provided valuable insights and guidance to procurement professionals at all levels, from early career professionals to seasoned procurement leaders. I also hope that it has helped to raise the profile and credibility of the procurement profession and highlight the critical role that procurement plays in driving business success. Thank you for joining me on this journey of discovery, and I wish you every success in your procurement career.

References:

Alpaydin, E. (2010). *Introduction to Machine Learning* (2nd ed.). Cambridge, MA: MIT Press.

Amodei, D., Olah, C., Steinhardt, J., Christiano, P., Schulman, J., & Mané, D. (2016). "Concrete Problems in AI Safety." arXiv preprint arXiv:1606.06565.

Antonopoulos, A. M. (2014). Mastering Bitcoin: Unlocking Digital Cryptocurrencies. O'Reilly Media.

Asimov, I. (1950). *I, Robot.* Gnome Press.

Atzori, L., Iera, A., & Morabito, G. (2017). "The internet of things: A survey." *Computer Networks*, 54(15), 2787-2805.

Beloglazov, A., & Abawajy, J. (2018). "Blockchain-based platforms: A survey of the research landscape." *Journal of Parallel and Distributed Computing*, 123, 9-27.

Berman, B. (2012). "3-D printing: The new industrial revolution." *Business Horizons*, 55(2), 155-162.

Bishop, C. M. (2006). "Pattern recognition and machine learning." Springer, New York.

Böhme, R., Christin, N., Edelman, B., & Moore, T. (2015). "Bitcoin: Economics, Technology, and Governance." *Journal of Economic Perspectives*, 29(2), 213-238.

Brynjolfsson, E., & McAfee, A. (2017). "The business of artificial intelligence." *Harvard Business Review.*

Brynjolfsson, E., & Mitchell, T. (2017). "What can machine learning do? Workforce implications." *Science*, 358(6370), 1530-1534.

Buterin, V. (2014). "A Next-Generation Smart Contract and Decentralized Application Platform." Ethereum Project.

Chen, M., Mao, S., & Liu, Y. (2014). "Big data: A survey." *Mobile Networks and Applications*, 19(2), 171-209.

Chen, Y., Li, H., Wang, X., & Wang, Y. (2019). "Machine learning for supply chain management: A review." *Computers & Industrial Engineering*, 128, 1011-1029.

Chopra, S., & Meindl, P. (2013). Supply Chain Management: Strategy, Planning, and Operation. Pearson Education Limited.

Chopra, S., & Meindl, P. (2016). *Supply Chain Management: Strategy, Planning, and Operation.* Pearson Education India.

Chui, M., Manyika, J., & Bughin, J. (2016). "The rise of AI." *McKinsey Quarterly.*

Crosby, M., Pattanayak, P., Verma, S., & Kalyanaraman, V. (2016). "Blockchain technology: beyond bitcoin." *Applied Innovation*, 2(6-10), 71-81.

Davenport, T. H., & Harris, J. G. (2007). *Competing on Analytics: The New Science of Winning.* Harvard Business Press.

David, E., & Weber, I. (2018). "Blockchain and the Economics of Crypto-tokens and Initial Coin Offerings." *Journal of Economic Perspectives*, 32(2), 157-178.

Domingos, P. (2018). The Master Algorithm: How the Quest for the Ultimate Learning Machine Will Remake Our World. Basic Books.

Engelberger, J. F. (1989). Robotics in Practice: Management and Applications of Robotics in Industry. Wiley-Interscience.

Fan, J., Li, Z., Zhao, Y., & Ma, Y. (2018). "Internet of things and its applications in supply chain management: A literature review." *Enterprise Information Systems*, 12(4), 464-490.

Fernandes, N., & Mateus, R. (2016). "The impact of 3D printing on the supply chain: Manufacturing and legal implications." *Computers in Industry*, 77, 1-12.

Floridi, L., & Cowls, J. (2019). "A unified framework of five principles for AI in society." *Harvard Data Science Review.*

Gartner. (2019). "Gartner Says Worldwide Supply Chain Management Market Grew 12.2% in 2018." https://www.gartner.com/en/newsroom/press-releases/2019-06-25-gartner-says-worldwide-supply-chain-management-market-grew-12-point-2-percent-in-2018

Ge, M., & Ou, J. (2019). "Blockchain technology and its industrial applications: A review." *Journal of Intelligent Manufacturing,* 30(2), 469-479.

Gershenfeld, N., & Cohen, S. (2017). "The internet of things and the future of manufacturing." *Foreign Affairs,* 96(1), 54-67.

Gibson, I., Rosen, D. W., & Stucker, B. (2015). "Additive manufacturing technologies: 3D printing, rapid prototyping, and direct digital manufacturing." Springer.

Goh, G. B., & Kong, W. C. (2019). "A Brief Survey of Deep Learning." *IEEE Transactions on Neural Networks and Learning Systems,* 30(12), 4341-4355.

Goodfellow, I., Bengio, Y., Courville, A., & Bengio, S. (2016). *Deep Learning.* MIT Press.

Gunasekaran, A., Papadopoulos, T., Dubey, R., Wamba, S. F., Childe, S. J., Hazen, B., ... & Akter, S. (2017). "The role of big data analytics in managing supply chain risks." *International Journal of Production Research,* 55(17), 5037-5052.

Gupta, A., & van der Laan, E. (2017). "Machine learning in supply chain management: A review." *Computers & Industrial Engineering,* 110, 21-42.

Gupta, M., & Kumar, U. (2020). "Procurement automation: An integrative review, classification and future directions."

Journal of Purchasing and Supply Management, 26(1), 100569.

Haeussinger, F., & Kuhn, M. (2018). "Robotics and supply chain management: a review of the literature and future implications." *International Journal of Production Research*, 56(8), 2767-2788.

Hastie, T., Tibshirani, R., & Friedman, J. (2009). *The Elements of Statistical Learning: Data Mining, Inference, and Prediction* (2nd ed.). Springer, New York.

Hinton, G. (2010). "Deep belief networks." *Scholarpedia*, 5(3), 5947.

Hinton, G., Deng, L., Yu, D., Dahl, G. E., Mohamed, A. R., Jaitly, N., ... & Kingsbury, B. (2012). "Deep neural networks for acoustic modeling in speech recognition: The shared views of four research groups." *IEEE Signal Processing Magazine*, 29(6), 82-97.

Huang, S. H., Liu, P., Mokasdar, A., & Hou, L. (2013). "Additive manufacturing and its societal impact: a literature review." *International Journal of Advanced Manufacturing Technology*, 67(5-8), 1191-1203.

Hugos, M. H. (2018). *Essentials of Supply Chain Management.* John Wiley & Sons.

IBM. (2019). "Procurement analytics: Uncover new opportunities and efficiencies." https://www.ibm.com/analytics/supply-chain-analytics/procurement-analytics

Ijomah, W., Childe, S. J., McMahon, C., & Newman, S. T. (2016). "Evaluating the benefits of 3D printing for sustainable supply chain management." *International Journal of Production Research*, 54(23), 7046-7060.

Jia, F., Sun, H., Lu, S., & Cai, X. (2016). The impact of 3D

Johnson, M. J., Khoshgoftaar, T. M., & Van Hulse, J. (2013). "Survey on deep learning with class imbalance." *Journal of Big Data,* 4(1), 27.

Jordan, M. I., & Mitchell, T. M. (2015). "Machine learning: Trends, perspectives, and prospects." *Science,* 349(6245), 255-260.

Kelleher, J. D., Tierney, B., & Tierney, B. (2018). *Data science: An introduction* (2nd ed.). Boca Raton, FL: CRC Press.

Khatib, O. (2008). "Robotics: challenges and future directions." *The Springer Handbook of Robotics* (pp. 3-20). Springer.

Khushaba, R. N., Kodagoda, S., & Lal, S. (2019). "The role of IoT-based systems in supply chain management: A review." *IEEE Systems Journal,* 13(2), 1290-1301.

KPMG. (2018). "The future of procurement: Leverage the power of procurement automation." KPMG International.

Krizhevsky, A., Sutskever, I., & Hinton, G. E. (2012). Imagenet.

Kshetri, N. (2018). "Blockchain's roles in meeting key supply chain management objectives." *International Journal of Information Management,* 39, 80-89.

Kusiak, A. (2019). "Robotics in supply chain management." *International Journal of Production Research,* 57(7), 2001-2014.

LeCun, Y., Bengio, Y., & Hinton, G. (2015). "Deep learning." *Nature,* 521(7553), 436-444.

Lee, H. L. (2004). "The triple-A supply chain." *Harvard business review,* 82(10), 102-112.

Lee, S., Lee, D., Lee, S., & Kim, S. (2019). "Blockchain-based secure and efficient data sharing for supply chain management of IoT." *Journal of Parallel and Distributed Computing,* 133, 99-107.

Li, S., Ragu-Nathan, T. S., Ragu-Nathan, B., & Subba Rao, S. (2006). "The impact of supply chain management practices on competitive advantage and organisational performance." *Omega*, 34(2), 107-124.

Li, S., Xu, L. D., & Wang, X. (2017). "IoT-based intelligent perception and access of manufacturing resource toward cloud manufacturing." *IEEE Transactions on Industrial Informatics*, 13(4), 1840-1848.

Lynch, K. M., & Park, F. C. (2017). *Modern Robotics: Mechanics, Planning, and Control.* Cambridge University Press.

Ma, L., Wang, X., & Shi, J. (2019). "Machine learning in supply chain management: a literature review." *International Journal of Production Research*, 57(7), 2179-2199.

Makhdoom, I., Hussain, M., Abbas, H., & Shah, T. A. (2019). "Blockchain applications: A review." *Journal of Network and Computer Applications*, 126, 50-70.

Mazzoli, A. (2017). 3D Printing: Technology, Applications, and Selection. CRC Press.

Microsoft. (2020). Procurement analytics. https://powerbi.microsoft.com/en-us/solutions/procurement-analytics/

Mistree, F., Rosen, D. W., & Schrage, D. P. (2017). "Smart use of manufacturing data: A review." *Journal of Manufacturing Systems*, 43, 217-228.

Mitchell, T. M. (1997). *Machine Learning.* McGraw Hill.

Monczka, R. M., Handfield, R. B., Giunipero, L. C., & Patterson, J. L. (2015). *Purchasing and Supply Chain Management*. Cengage Learning.

Möser, M., & Böhme, R. (2018). "A survey on security attacks and countermeasures in blockchain-based applications." *IEEE Access*, 6, 13423-13449.

Murphy, K. P. (2012). *Machine Learning: A Probabilistic Perspective.* Cambridge, MA: MIT Press.

Murr, L. E., Gaytan, S. M., Medina, F., Lopez, H., Martinez, E., Machado, B. I., ... & Wicker, R. B

Nakamoto, S. (2008). "Bitcoin: A peer-to-peer electronic cash system." Bitcoin.org.

Narayanan, A., Bonneau, J., Felten, E., Miller, A., & Goldfeder, S. (2016). *Bitcoin and Cryptocurrency Technologies: A Comprehensive Introduction.* Princeton University Press.

Ng, A. (2017). "Machine learning yearning." Technical report, Stanford University.

O'Reilly, T. (2010). "What is data science?" O'Reilly Media, Inc.

Oracle. (2021). Procurement analytics. https://www.oracle.com/solutions/procurement-analytics/

PwC. (2019). "Procurement's next frontier: Automation." PwC Global.

Raschka, S., & Mirjalili, V. (2021). *Python Machine Learning* (3rd ed.). Packt Publishing Ltd.

Rengier, F., Mehndiratta, A., von Tengg-Kobligk, H., Zechmann, C. M., Unterhinninghofen, R., Kauczor, H. U., & Giesel, F. L. (2010). "3D printing based on imaging data: review of medical applications." *International Journal of Computer Assisted Radiology and Surgery*, 5(4), 335-341.

Robotics Online. (n.d.). Applications of Robotics. https://www.robotics.org/applications.

Robotics Online. (n.d.). Challenges in Robotics. https://www.robotics.org/challenges.

Russakovsky, O., Deng, J., Su, H., Krause, J., Satheesh, S., Ma, S., ... & Berg, A. C. (2015). "ImageNet large scale visual recognition challenge." *International Journal of Computer Vision*, 115(3), 211-252.

Russell, S. J., & Norvig, P. (2010). *Artificial Intelligence: A Modern Approach* (3rd ed.). Upper Saddle River, NJ: Prentice Hall.

Rüßmann, M., Lorenz, M., Gerbert, P., Waldner, M., Justus, J., Engel, P., & Harnisch, M. (2015). "Industry 4.0: the future of productivity and growth in manufacturing industries." *Boston Consulting Group*, 9(1), 1-24.

SAP. (2021). Procurement analytics. https://www.sap.com/products/procurement-analytics.html

Shah, S. A. A., Hussain, M., & Hussain, S. A. (2018). "An IoT-based smart logistics system for supply chain management." *Journal of Ambient Intelligence and Humanized Computing*, 9(4), 1137-115

Shalev-Shwartz, S., & Ben-David, S. (2014). *Understanding Machine Learning: From Theory to Algorithms.* Cambridge, MA: Cambridge University Press.

Silver, D., Huang, A., Maddison, C. J., Guez, A., Sifre, L., Van Den Driessche, G., ... & Dieleman, S. (2016). "Mastering the game of Go with deep neural networks and tree search." *Nature*, 529(7587), 484-489.

Silver, D., Schrittwieser, J., Simonyan, K., Antonoglou, I., Huang, A., Guez, A., ... & Petersen, S. (2018). "A general reinforcement learning algorithm that masters chess, shogi, and go through self-play." *Science*, 362(6419), 1140-1144.

Singamneni, S., & Adepu, R. (2017). "Review on recent advancements in 3D printing." *Journal of Mechanical Engineering Research and Developments*, 40(2), 80-85.

Sourcing Force. (2021). "Procurement automation: What it is and why it's important." https://www.sourcing-force.com/en/procurement-automation/

SpendEdge. (2020). Procurement automation market – Procurement intelligence report. https://www.spendedge.com/store/procurement-intelligence/procurement-automation-market-procurement-intelligence-report

Srinivasan, A. (2018). "Procurement Analytics: Unlocking the Benefits." https://www.oracle.com/industries/process-manufacturing/procurement-analytics-unlocking-benefits.pdf

Sutskever, I., Vinyals, O., & Le, Q. V. (2014). "Sequence to sequence learning with neural networks. Advances in neural information processing systems." 3104-3112.

Swan, M. (2015). Blockchain: Blueprint for a New Economy. O'Reilly Media.

Swan, M. (2017). "Blockchain thinking: The brain as a decentralized autonomous corporation." *IEEE Technology and Society Magazine*, 36(2), 41-52.

Tableau. (2020). "Procurement analytics." https://www.tableau.com/solutions/workbook/procurement-analytics-workbook

Tapscott, D., & Tapscott, A. (2016). Blockchain Revolution: How the Technology Behind Bitcoin is Changing Money, Business, and the World. Penguin.

Thrun, S., & Burgard, W. (2005). *Probabilistic Robotics*. MIT Press.

Tiggemann, M. (2017). Procurement Analytics. In Predictive Analytics: The Power to Predict Who Will Click, Buy, Lie, or Die (pp. 233-246). John Wiley & Sons.

Topol, E. J. (2019). "High-performance medicine: the convergence of human and artificial intelligence." *Nature Medicine*, 25(1), 44-56.

Verma, A., & Verter, V. (2018). "Machine learning in support of supply chain management: A review of the state of the art." *International Journal of Production Research*, 56(1-2), 89-119.

Verma, D., & Dutta, D. (2018). "Impact of predictive analytics in supply chain management." *International Journal of Engineering & Technology*, 7(3.26), 384-386.

Wang, C. C., Lin, J. C., & Huang, Y. C. (2018). "3D printing technologies for tissue engineering applications." *In Tissue Engineering and Regenerative Medicine* (pp. 207-226). Springer.

Weng, J., McClelland, J., Pentland, A., Sporns, O., Stock

Yamins, D. L., & DiCarlo, J. J. (2016). "Using goal-driven deep learning models to understand sensory cortex." *Nature Neuroscience*, 19(3), 356-365.

Yang, Y., Chen, Y., Wang, C., & Wu, H. (2018). "The challenges and opportunities of 3D printing for cardiovascular disease." *Advanced Healthcare Materials*, 7(4), 1701167.

Yoon, S., Lee, J., & Kim, D. (2018). "An empirical study of the impact of procurement analytics on procurement performance." *Journal of Purchasing and Supply Management*, 24(1), 1-9.

Zeng, L., Zhou, X., & Shi, Y. (2019). "Smart warehousing for intelligent logistics: A case study of a 3PL company." *IEEE Transactions on Industrial Informatics*, 15(6), 3497-3507.

Zhang, Y., Wen, J., & Zhu, H. (2018). "Blockchain-based data management and analytics for customer-driven intelligent services." *IEEE Transactions on Services Computing*, 11(1), 48-62.

Zhang, Y., Yuan, Z., & Liu, C. (2018). "3D printing technology: a review on its recent progress and future prospects." *Engineering*, 4(5), 729-742.

Zheng, Y., & Chen, H. (2019). "Machine learning for supply chain management: A review and future research directions." *International Journal of Production Research*, 57(7), 2053-2074.

Zheng, Z., Xie, S., Dai, H., Chen, X., & Wang, H. (2017). "Blockchain challenges and opportunities: A survey." *International Journal of Web and Grid Services*, 13(4), 352-375.

Zohar, A. (2015). "Bitcoin: under the hood." *Communications of the ACM*, 58(9), 104-113.

Zondag, J., Roos, J., & Kumar, A. (2017). "Procurement analytics: Enabling insights, driving value." *Deloitte Insights*. https://www2.deloitte.com/us/en/insights/focus/cognitive-technologies/procurement-analytics-enabling-insights-driving-value.html

Zorzetto, D. (2019). "The Future of Procurement Analytics." *Supply Chain Brain*. https://www.supplychainbrain.com/articles/30163-the-future-of-procurement-analytics

www.ingramcontent.com/pod-product-compliance
Lightning Source LLC
Chambersburg PA
CBHW052344220526
45465CB00003BA/953